O9-ABH-032

Analytical Reading Inventory

Third Edition

Mary Lynn Woods
Reading Specialist
Orchard Country Day School
Indianapolis, Indiana

Alden J. Moe
Louisiana State University

Charles E. Merrill Publishing Company
A Bell & Howell Company
Columbus   Toronto   London   Sydney

Analytical Reading Inventory

Third Edition

Mary Lynn Woods
Reading Consultant
Eagle-Union Community School Corporation
Zionsville, Indiana

Alden J. Moe
Louisiana State University

87-1270

Charles E. Merrill Publishing Company
A Bell & Howell Company
Columbus   Toronto   London   Sydney

Published by
Charles E. Merrill Publishing Co.
A Bell & Howell Company
Columbus, Ohio 43216

This book was set in News Gothic.
Production Coordination: Ben Shriver
Copy Editor: Holly Bardoe
Cover Design Coordination: Cathy Watterson
Cover Photos: Strix Pix

Library of Congress Catalog Card Number: 84-61847
International Standard Book Number: 0–675–20319–8
Printed in the United States of America
3   4   5   6   7   8   9   10–90   89   88   87   86

PREFACE

The *Analytical Reading Inventory,* third edition, is a diagnostic instrument intended for use by the prospective teacher, the classroom teacher, or the reading specialist in the observation, recording, and analysis of a student's reading performance. We believe that the diagnosing of reading ability is one of the most important responsibilities assigned to the teacher and that careful assessment leads to improved instruction. We believe also that the use of the *Analytical Reading Inventory* will enable teachers to identify the student's level of word recognition, determine strengths and weaknesses in word recognition and comprehension, identify levels of reading achievement, and find the level of potential for reading growth.

We feel that once the procedures used in informal diagnosis are fully understood, the teacher will become confident in using this method of assessment and will be reassured that a thorough analysis is being accomplished. It is our profound hope that users of this instrument will find it a convenient, efficient, and accurate tool with which to accomplish the many tasks of informal assessment.

The first edition of the *Analytical Reading Inventory* has proven to be a useful guide for practicing teachers, as well as college and university students enrolled in courses on the diagnosis and correction of reading problems. This new edition provides further assistance for administering and interpreting the Inventory, including expanded instructions and a sample of a student's reading performance and consequent instructional recommendations.

We express our gratitude to the many individuals involved in the development of this inventory. A sincere thank you goes to Dr. Helen Felsenthal who encouraged the first author to undertake this project, and to Ken, John and Katherine Woods who faithfully stuck by the first author through the ARI's completion. To Michael Igo and Anna Sanford for their field testing the inventory with undergraduates, for their use of the inventory in a clinical setting, and for their constructive suggestions for changes, we are most appreciative. To Gloria Brown and Cynthia Pulver for the time and energy expended in analyzing the passages, we are thankful. And to Joan Gipe for field testing the inventory with her undergraduates, for her assistance in determining the readability levels of the passages, and her ability to see that the second author completed his assignments on time, we offer special thanks.

We wish to express our sincere appreciation to Dr. Katherine E. Richmond, University of Florida, Dr. Susan Homan, University of South Florida, Dr. Ellen Garfinkel, University of Virginia, Dr. Bonnie Chambers, Bowling Green State University, Dr. Sharon Wooden, New Mexico State University, and Dr. Doris E. Jakubek, Central Washington University, who provided valuable feedback prior to the preparation of the third edition. And finally, to Vicki Knight and Merrill editors for their continued support, we thank you especially for your thoroughness and patience.

DEDICATION

In memory of A. EDSON SMITH,
a dedicated educator and father
of the first author of this text.

Also in memory of SISTER MARY EDWARD DOLAN, PBVM,
who helped the second author construct
his first informal reading inventory.

And to all those other professionals who
are committed to helping children read.

CONTENTS

FORM B

FORM C

HOW TO USE THIS INVENTORY

For those individuals who intend to use this inventory for assessing the reading performance of students, it is recommended that the entire inventory be read carefully, including the graded passages and the comprehension questions. Since many individuals who use this inventory will be familiar with informal assessment procedures, the information listed below, concerning the contents of each major section, is presented to permit greater efficiency in using the inventory.

Introduction

The introduction presents *general* background information on the nature, content, and use of informal reading inventories. Information concerning the use of the word *analytical* for this particular inventory is also presented. This section is recommended reading for all users of the inventory.

Organization

The organization of the word lists and passages to be used with the student is discussed in this section. Since inventories differ in their organization, this section is also recommended reading for all users of the inventory.

Development and Validation

All matters relating to the development and validation of the inventory are presented in this section. Specifically, the writing of the student passages, the development of the comprehension questions, the various analyses which were conducted on the passages to insure continuity in readability, and the field testing with students are all presented in some detail. Also in this section is descriptive statistical information concerning the nature of the graded passages. This section is recommended reading for persons interested in readability and the computer assisted analysis of language. It is *not*, however, essential reading for all users of the inventory.

Instructions

Since this section deals specifically with the use of this inventory, a careful reading is recommended, even for those acquainted with the use of reading inventories.

Student Passages

It is essential that users of this inventory read and become thoroughly familiar with the passages before they are used for student assessment. Once a particular form (A, B, or C) has been selected for student use, all passages contained in that form should be read carefully. It is also essential that the teacher's copy of the passage, the accompanying introductory background information, and the comprehension questions be carefully read before they are used for diagnosis.

Student and Class Record Summary Sheets

The use of the various summary sheets contained in this inventory is discussed under "Instructions."

References

The last section of the inventory contains three sets of references. The first set includes selected references on corrective and remedial reading instruction. The second set includes the references which have been cited in various sections of the inventory, and the last set includes the references which provided the background information necessary to write the student passages. While none of these three sets of references is essential, users of the inventory may find the first one of help in developing an instructional plan after the diagnosis.

INTRODUCTION

The *Analytical Reading Inventory* (ARI) has been developed to assist teachers, reading specialists, and prospective teachers in analyzing the reading performance of students in grades two through nine. It is somewhat similar to the informal reading inventories (IRIs) teachers made by compiling a series of graded passages; these inventories were then used informally in their classrooms. Most informal reading inventories contain a series of graded passages from the first-grade level through the sixth-grade level, at least, and a series of questions corresponding to the graded passages with which the teacher checks the student's comprehension of the passage read. Sometimes IRIs have more than one series of graded passages. Generally, IRIs are used individually with students. Though they have been used since the 1940s, IRIs have become more popular in the last decade because of the publication, *Informal Reading Inventories* (Johnson & Kress, 1965).

The *Analytical Reading Inventory* is an informal reading inventory. Because of the care given to the development of the graded passages, the questions for checking comprehension, and the instructions for use, users of the ARI may place greater faith in their analysis of the reading task than with IRIs presently available.

The word **analytical** was selected because it means examining the component parts separately or in relationship to the whole. With the *Analytical Reading Inventory*, teachers will have a tool which will enable them to look at specific reading behaviors and yet observe the reading act as a whole.

Specifically, the ARI is designed to be used individually in order to enable the teacher to do the following:

1. Identify a general level of word recognition
2. Identify strengths and weaknesses in word recognition skills
3. Examine performance in oral and/or silent reading
4. Examine comprehension strategies
5. Find the independent reading level
6. Find the instructional reading level
7. Find the frustration reading level
8. Find the reading capacity or listening level

ORGANIZATION

The parts of the ARI which are to be used in assessing reading skills consist of a series of graded word lists and a series of graded passages (sometimes referred to as **selections**). With both the word lists and the passages, there are student booklet copies and teacher record copies. The student will read from the student booklet, and the teacher will make notations concerning the reading on the teacher record forms or on a reproduced copy.[1]

There are seven word lists for each form, with each list containing twenty words. They are graded as follows:

> primer
> first grade
> second grade
> third grade
> fourth grade
> fifth grade
> sixth grade

For each of the three forms, there are ten passages graded as follows:

> primer
> first grade
> second grade
> third grade
> fourth grade
> fifth grade
> sixth grade
> seventh grade
> eighth grade
> ninth grade

The teacher may use any of the three forms (A, B, or C) since they are equivalent forms, and one may be used independently of the other two.

---

[1]Permission is granted by the publisher to reproduce the teacher record forms and the summary sheets.

DEVELOPMENT AND VALIDATION

The development of the *Analytical Reading Inventory* took place over a two-year period and included writing, field testing, computer analyses, and several revisions of thirty original passages. This section contains information concerning the content of the graded passages, the nature of the comprehension questions, the procedures used for establishing the readability of the passages and the equivalency of the forms, and the field testing of the inventory with elementary and junior high school students. Finally, a discussion of the criteria used for the identification of the various reading levels is presented.

Passage Content

One of the objectives was to prepare original writings which were motivational for both boys and girls and also nonsexist in nature. Therefore, a considerable amount of effort was expended learning about the reading interests of students at varying grade levels. Such sources as *Children and Books* (Arbuthnot & Sutherland, 1972), *The New York Times Report on Teenage Reading Tastes and Habits* (Freiberger, 1973), *Reading Interests of Children and Young Adults* (Kujoth, 1970), and *Reading Children's Books and Our Pluralistic Society* (Tanyzer & Karl, 1972) provided information which influenced the content and style of the selections in the ARI.

The situations depicted in the passages are actions and events corresponding with children's feelings so that the reader may perceive himself or herself in the situation, maintain empathy with the principal character in the selection, or be held by fascination of the mysterious. The passage topics were carefully selected to appeal to both boys and girls.

In addition, the content of the passages is consistent across all three forms. For example, all passages at the sixth-grade level deal with famous scientists or inventors who developed some life-saving technique or device. Because both content, which affects the reader's motivational appeal, and readability are consistent, two major variables which influence a student's performance are controlled. This becomes a major factor in reassessment and also in the comparison of oral and silent reading comprehension.

While the passages were not written with a controlled vocabulary, the careful selection of words had to be a factor in the creation of the passages. Therefore, word selection was guided in some cases by the graded word lists contained in *Basic Elementary Reading Vocabularies* (Harris & Jacobson, 1972).

Comprehension Questions

One of the major difficulties in the construction of informal reading inventories lies in devising questions with which to assess the reader's understanding of a passage. The prime concern in devising such questions is that they are passage dependent. The development of the questions was influenced by the work of Sanders (1966), Tuinman (1971), and Valmont (1972).

The questions used to measure comprehension in the ARI are of six types. They are listed with their parenthetical abbreviations as follows:

1. Main idea (mi)
2. Factual (f)
3. Terminology (t)
4. Cause and effect (ce)
5. Inferential (inf)
6. Conclusion (con)

The first type of question, main idea (mi), was developed to insure that the child derived the major focus of the passage. This question was designed in either an open-ended fashion revealing no facts or clues, or in a form where the reader was given *some* facts. The choice depended upon the complexity of the text.

The second type of question, factual (f), calls for facts which have been explicitly stated in the text. This type of question deals with only literal understanding.

The terminology (t) question is the only question which may or may not be completely text related. A terminology question may be text related because clues are given in the passage to aid the reader in deriving the meaning of the word or phrase. For example, the question, "What is meant by the word *challenger*?" is asked. The text states, "Look out, Sheila Young thought as she saw her challenger's bicycle come too close. At that moment a horrifying thing happened as she was bumped by another racer at forty miles an hour." In the second sentence a clue is given which will help the student derive the meaning of the word *challenger*.

On the other hand, in the text, "At dawn Jody awakened to the banging of the barn door," the question, "What is meant by the phrase, *at dawn*?" is raised. In this sentence and the subsequent text there is no clue to the meaning of the phrase, *at dawn*. This response requires the student to draw upon his or her background knowledge to demonstrate an understanding of the phrase.

Cause and effect questions (ce) require the reader to see relationships between facts given in the text. These questions are constructed so that the examiner provides either the cause or the effect, and the student is asked to supply the other.

Inferential (inf) questions require that the pupil infer a judgment or a deduction based on the facts stated in the text. In the ARI, an inferential question calls for the pupil to take *one* fact from the passage and deduct or infer his or her own conclusion. A conclusion (con) question requires that the pupil derive an answer from *two or more* facts stated in the passage. Thus, the distinction is made between these two types of questions.

Establishing the Reading Levels

Grade level validation of the reading level of each passage was established through the use of readability formulas and computer analyses of the text. The readability formulas provided grade level readability estimates for each of the passages, whereas the computer analyses provided specific information such as vocabulary diversity and syntactic complexity on the language used in each passage. Such procedures were used to assure that subsequent passages within a form increased in difficulty and also to assure that passages at a specific grade level were comparable among the three forms.

The revised Spache formula (Spache, 1974) was used to calculate the readability estimates for passages at the primer through grade three levels, and the Harris-Jacobson Formula 2 (Harris & Sipay, 1975) was used for levels four through nine. The readability estimates yielded by the Spache formula for the primary levels (primer—three) are summarized in Table I, and those yielded by the Harris-Jacobson formula for the intermediate grades and junior high (four—nine) are summarized in Table II. Since the Harris-Jacobson formula yields a predicted score which must be converted to a readability level, both the predicted score and the readability level are shown.

TABLE I

Spache readability results for primary levels

Grade Level	Form A Score	Form B Score	Form C Score
Primer	1.5	1.5	1.5
One	1.7	1.7	1.8
Two	2.5	2.4	2.5
Three	3.2	3.4	3.1

TABLE II

Harris-Jacobson readability results for intermediate and junior high levels

Grade Level	Form A		Form B		Form C	
	Predicted Score	Readability Level	Predicted Score	Readability Level	Predicted Score	Readability Level
four	4.78	four	4.73	four	4.63	four
five	5.61	six	4.85	five	4.98	five
six	6.07	seven[a]	5.79	seven[a]	6.27	seven[a]
seven	5.88	seven[a]	5.58	six	5.98	seven[a]
eight	7.44	eight +[a]	7.08	eight +[a]	8.29	eight +[a]
nine	7.78	eight +[a]	7.26	eight +[a]	8.02	eight +[a]

[a]Scores provided are based on extrapolation. See Harris and Sipay (1975) for further information.

Caution must be expressed to those who would conclude, on the basis of the information presented in Table II, that level six of Form A, for example, is more difficult than level seven. The results of readability formulas provide estimates; they are imprecise, but they do provide a gauge for comparing text.

Because a number of factors determine the extent to which a passage is or is not readable, additional analyses of the student passages were conducted. One of these analyses was an examination of the vocabulary diversity of each passage. Vocabulary diversity is the extent to which the vocabulary items, the words, differ within a text. For example, a 100 word passage written with 100 *different* words is more diverse than a 100 word passage written with only 20 *different* words. Factors used to compute a vocabulary diversity score for each passage—the total number of words and the number of different words contained in each passage—together with the vocabulary diversity scores are summarized in Table III.[2]

TABLE III

Number of total words, number of different words, and vocabulary diversity score for each level of Forms A, B, and C

Level	Number of Total Words			Number of Different Words			Vocabulary Diversity Score		
	A	B	C	A	B	C	A	B	C
Primer	50	50	50	25	26	34	2.5	2.6	3.4
One	79	77	76	41	55	42	3.3	4.4	3.4
Two	118	113	118	71	77	78	4.6	5.1	5.1
Three	143	138	148	86	94	88	5.1	5.7	5.1
Four	144	157	144	96	96	87	5.7	5.4	5.1
Five	171	197	192	116	120	104	6.3	6.0	5.3
Six	192	186	189	115	123	117	5.9	6.4	6.0
Seven	262	235	240	148	150	145	6.5	6.9	6.6
Eight	286	283	257	170	179	172	7.1	7.5	7.6
Nine	339	321	315	200	190	197	7.7	7.5	7.8

The information presented in Table III shows that there is consistency within levels and that, generally, there is an increase in the length of the passages from one level to the next. There is also consistency with the number of different words contained in each passage within a grade level, and, in the most cases, there is an increase as the grade level increases. The vocabulary diversity scores also show consistency within grade level, and with few exceptions there is an increase in the vocabulary diversity as the grade level increases.

Another measure of the difficulty of text may be gained by examining sentence length. Although sentence length was a factor in determining the readability estimates, the average sentence length and the longest sentences contained within each passage are also presented as evidence that there is both grade level consistency *and* a progression of difficulty from levels primer through nine. Information on sentence length is summarized in Table IV.

---

[2] The technical term for this score is **type-token ratio.** Because the passages varied in length, a corrected type-token ratio was calculated where the number of different words was divided by the square root of two times the total number of words.

Development and Validation

TABLE IV

Average sentence length and longest sentence for all passages

	Average Sentence Length			Longest Sentence		
	A	B	C	A	B	C
Primer	6.3	6.3	6.3	8	9	11
One	8.8	8.6	8.4	13	11	11
Two	9.1	9.4	9.8	13	16	17
Three	11.9	11.5	12.3	25	20	21
Four	11.1	12.1	12.0	17	26	17
Five	13.2	16.4	16.0	24	34	27
Six	16.0	15.5	14.5	23	19	23
Seven	18.7	15.7	16.0	37	26	31
Eight	19.1	17.7	17.1	39	29	34
Nine	18.8	17.8	18.5	39	28	30

The figures presented in Table IV show that the grade level increases as the average sentence length increases. Similarly, the longest sentence contained within a passage is *likely* to be longer as the grade level increases.

The information presented in Tables III and IV should be *used with* and *compared to* the readability estimate figures presented in Tables I and II. The authors believe that the combined information supports the conviction that the grade levels assigned to the specific passages are valid and that there is consistency within a given grade level for all three forms. It is realized, however, that readability is content related and the final test as to whether a passage can be read and comprehended is to have it read by those *for whom it is intended*. Therefore, extensive field testing with elementary and junior high school students was also undertaken.

Field Testing

A delineation of all the steps which led to the field testing with students is difficult because at various stages in the development of the inventory some portions were partially tested and revised prior to the field testing. For example, if doubt arose concerning the content or the wording of a specific passage, it was "tried out" on school-age children. A similar procedure was used with the comprehension questions. Often the advice of classroom teachers and reading specialists was solicited when a particularly troublesome problem arose.

Finally, the ARI needed field testing by individuals unassociated with its development. This testing was accomplished by having approximately 80 advanced undergraduate students (in their second course on reading instruction) use it to assess the reading skills of approximately 200 students in grades two through eight. The users of the inventory were asked to pay particular attention to (1) the appropriateness of the directions for its use, (2) the motivational appeal of the respective passages, (3) any ambiguities in the passages or the questions, and (4) the extent to which the comprehension questions were passage dependent.

Results of the field testing showed the major problem to be with the comprehension questions, and many were subsequently revised. Directions on how to make use of the results were also improved by including a qualitative summary sheet of student performance. Field testing also indicated that some passages were too difficult, and they were rewritten at an easier reading level. Finally, the passages and the questions were sent to Charles E. Merrill Publishing for editing, and then the final readability checks and computer analyses of the text were conducted.

Criteria for Determining Levels

One of the main purposes of the ARI is to establish reading levels for a student. Therefore, the criteria used for determining these levels becomes important. The criteria long used to establish the informal reading inventory levels have generally been attributed to Betts (Beldin, 1970; Pikulski, 1974). However, Powell (1970) and Powell and Dunkeld (1971) have suggested that the numerical standard used for determining the instructional level is too stringent, particularly at lower levels.

In an attempt to determine whether the Betts criteria or the Powell criteria were more appropriate, Pikulski (1974) reports contradictory findings. While users of the inventory should consider Powell's advice that the 95% word recognition score used for determining the instructional level may be too high for primary grade students, they should also realize that Ekwall (1976a, 1976b) presents strong evidence that the Betts criteria should be maintained. Therefore, the criteria used to determine the three reading levels and the listening levels are those traditionally used and identified (the Betts criteria) in *Informal Reading Inventories* (Johnson & Kress, 1965). These criteria are enumerated in detail on pages 12-19, and all scoring guides in the ARI are based on them.

INSTRUCTIONS

Because the inventory is used to identify specific reading strengths, weaknesses, and levels of reading achievement, it is necessary to have a systematic method of examining and recording the student's reading behavior. The method most often used is to note the mispronunciations (referred to as **miscues**) as the student reads orally and to assess the student's comprehension immediately after the passage has been read. Careful administration of the inventory can determine the reading level at which the student can function independently, the level—or levels—at which the student should be instructed, the level at which frustration negates understanding, and the listening (reading capacity) level.

The following sections present a discussion of quantitative and qualitative analysis; identify the types of questions used for evaluating comprehension strengths and weaknesses; show the criteria for establishing each of the reading levels; discuss oral and silent reading; and present a step-by-step procedure for administering the ARI.

Quantitative and Qualitative Analysis

Generally, users of informal reading inventories have relied upon a system of coding oral reading where all deviations from the text have been tabulated. This procedure has also been referred to as a quantitative analysis (Pikulski, 1974), since deviations were simply counted and a score was computed. In recent years the word **miscue** has become popular (Goodman, 1973; Goodman & Burke, 1972). A miscue is defined as a deviation from the text. However, not all miscues occur consistently in a student's reading behavior or are indicative of a serious reading problem. In order to gain a comprehensive analysis of a student's reading behavior, it is beneficial to analyze miscues qualitatively as well as quantitatively. In order to effectively do this the examiner must determine if the miscue occurs consistently and/or alters the meaning of the text.

For example, if a student substitutes the word *the* for *a*, indicating no change in the meaning of the text, the miscue is not as severe as the substitution of the word *read* for *think*. In order to best document patterns in a student's reading behavior, the examiner's major concern is to determine if the miscues occur consistently throughout a reading passage, and if they are the type of deviations which change the meaning of the text.

In this inventory, two sheets have been provided for summarizing the information gained from observing a student's reading behavior. The completion of the Student Record Summary Sheet renders a quantitative view, and the Qualitative Analysis Summary Sheet provides a qualitative analysis.

Retellings

A thorough retelling gives information about the characters and the schematic structure of the plot, thus helping the examiner to know if the reader is able to adequately interpret the author's message. This analysis provides the necessary information to help the examiner determine the adequacy of the reader's comprehension, and predict whether the reader's current language development will match an author's language usage. Directions for administering and evaluating a retelling, and recommendations for giving and scoring comprehension questions are found in this section, page 16, Step 4.

Comprehension Questions

A definition of each of the types of comprehension questions and the rationale for the use of each was discussed previously. However, the major concern in the development of the questions for each passage was that they be passage dependent; that is, the successful answering of a comprehension question should be based upon information gained from reading the passage rather than information the student had acquired from previous experiences. With the exception of some of the terminology questions, it is felt that comprehension questions for the ARI are passage dependent.[3]

The following types of comprehension questions are included in the ARI (see p. 6 for a detailed description):

1. Main idea (mi)
2. Factual (f)
3. Terminology (t)
4. Cause and effect (ce)
5. Inferential (inf)
6. Conclusions (con)

When a student answers a question incompletely or inaccurately, the examiner must try to determine if there is some kind of pattern to the student's response. For example, some students may be able to answer the factual and terminology questions well but may have difficulty with the inferential and conclusion questions. Such an observation by the teacher has important implications for instruction.

---

[3]Anderson (1977) provides further verification of the passage dependency of the comprehension questions.

Determining the Reading Levels

The reading behavior associated with each reading level and a means of assessing oral reading are presented in the following sections.

Independent Level

This is the level at which the student can read with no more than one uncorrected miscue in each 100 words (99%) and with at least 90% comprehension. In some cases, the students reading at this level *may exceed* the above criterion for miscues if comprehension is maintained at the 90% level or higher. At the independent level, the student's reading is fluent and expressive with accurate observation of punctuation; the student recognizes the print with confidence.

Instructional Level

This is the level at which the student can read no more than five uncorrected miscues in 100 words (95%) and with at least 75% comprehension. In some cases, at this level, the student's reading may exceed the above criterion for miscues if comprehension is maintained at a higher level. At the instructional level, the student's reading is generally expressive though he or she reads more slowly than at the independent level.

Frustration Level

This is the level beyond which reading has little meaning. It may be thought of as the "breakdown point." Miscues exceed 10% (less than 90% correct) with comprehension about 50%. At this level, the student exhibits obvious frustration because the material is too difficult. Except for an occasional brief testing period, no child should be expected to read at this level.

Listening Level

This level is sometimes referred to as the hearing comprehension level, the hearing capacity level, or the reading potential level. It is the level at which the student can comprehend 75% of the materials read aloud by the examiner. This level provides an estimate of the child's reading potential and becomes important when it is compared with the instructional level.

Oral Reading

It is important to learn as much as possible about the student's knowledge of vocabulary, word recognition skills, and inefficient reading habits as the student reads orally. The examiner should be recording all deviations from the text. The kinds of miscues which should be observed and a method of recording them is presented in Table V (p. 14).

TABLE V

Type of Deviation from the Text	Recorded Example
Omission: Circle the word or punctuation mark omitted.	Jack lost his (brother's) bike.
Insertions: Write the inserted word or words.	Mary was not ^very happy.
Substitutions: Write the word substituted.	The ~~horse~~ house trotted along the road.
Aided Words: Draw a line through the word pronounced for the student. (An examiner should aid words for a reader as seldom as possible.)	Mark began to ~~tremble~~.
Repetitions: Record only if two or more words are repeated.	Chris is <u>serious about her</u> career.
Reversals: Use curved lines to indicate words or letters reversed.	He lay exhausted on the ground.
Hesitation: Use a slash (/) to denote improper hesitation. Do not count as miscues.	That was no/laughing matter.

If a student makes a miscue or some other deviation from the text but self-corrects, it should be recorded as self-correction (SC). A self-correction should *not* be a counted miscue. It should be noted that a reader who self-corrects is one who is monitoring the meaning. Some examples of recorded self-corrections follow:

An old beaver dam from upstream broke.
SC boys

No one could enter the tunnel.
SC

Silent Reading

There are some students who will comprehend a passage better when they read silently rather than orally. If the examiner feels the student should read a passage silently, alternate forms are provided in which selections of equivalent levels may be used. Examiner judgment in this situation might be based upon the following:

1. The reader is self-conscious and not relaxed when reading aloud.
2. The reader's major word recognition miscues are repetitions, and the examiner feels that a silent reading passage may render a more accurate analysis of the student's comprehension skills.

Using the Inventory with a Student

The inventory should be used in an atmosphere that is relaxed and informal. If the examiner and student are newly acquainted, time should be spent to establish rapport before the reading begins. It is recommended that the student be informed that the examiner will be taking brief notes during the administration of the inventory. Some users of the inventory will find it valuable to tape record the entire session; this enables them to check their notations later. If a tape recorder *is* used, it should not hamper the student's performance. Therefore, the use should be planned and the operation nondistracting. The following steps suggest the sequence to be used.

Have the student begin reading the words in the primer isolated word list from the form you have selected. As the student says each word, note the pronunciation and record appropriately on the teacher record form. Mark a plus (+) if the word is pronounced correctly. If the word is incorrectly pronounced, write the word the student said. If the student did not know the word, mark DK, and if the student self-corrects a miscue, mark SC next to the word corrected.

Step 1

Continue until the student misses (mispronounces or does not know) five of the twenty words in a list. In any list, stop at the point where the fifth word is missed unless the student expresses a strong desire to finish the list.

After the student has completed reading several lists, it is suggested that the examiner ask the student to use some randomly selected words from a list in a complete sentence. For example, the examiner might say, "Place number fifteen from list three in a sentence." It is also suggested that these sentences be written down on the corresponding teacher's record. This procedure will help the examiner to readily identify a student who might be a "word caller" (one who pronounces words correctly, but who has no concept of the meaning or knowledge of its proper use in context). Also, the procedure will facilitate the selection of the appropriate reading passage.

The next step, the oral reading, should be started at the highest level at which the student correctly pronounced all twenty words on a list. In some instances, where only one word was mispronounced, for example, the examiner may decide to start at a higher level. However, if in doubt as to where to start the oral reading, begin at the lower level.

Open the booklet to a student passage corresponding to the highest level at which the child successfully pronounced and used appropriately in context all words in a word list.

Step 2

It is recommended that the evaluator read carefully all examiner's introductions, passages, and questions prior to the administration of the ARI to insure complete familiarity with the inventory. Most of the examiner's introductions are included to provide the evaluator with the necessary background for the passage. It is suggested that as little cueing as possible be given to the student prior to the reading, therefore, most examiner's introductions need not be read to the student. However, if the evaluator feels that the student may be confused while reading the passage without some sort of an introduction, it is appropriate to include one. For example, the examiner might say: "Please read the following story. It is about something which happened many years ago. Sometimes, a long time ago, a school teacher might live with a student's family."

Before the student begins to read, tell him/her that after the passage is read, you will ask for a retelling and possibly some comprehension questions. As the student reads from the student passage, record oral reading miscues on the corresponding teacher's passage. After the student has read aloud, take the booklet from the reader before assessing the comprehension.

Step 3

Step 4

After the passage has been read ask the reader to retell the text. The examiner should record the retelling in the space provided on the Teacher Record Sheet. A complete retelling will include:

1. A listing of the characters, a description of the characters, or both
2. Reference to the time and setting of the passage, if applicable
3. A description of the plot or events told according to the author's sequence and logic
4. A summarization of the main idea

After the reader has told all that he/she intends to tell, the examiner may probe for further information. As a final probe to determine the reader's ability to summarize the main ideas, the examiner should say, "In one or two short sentences, tell me what this passage is about."

If a retelling is thorough, the examiner may choose not to ask any of the comprehension questions, or just select a few, such as vocabulary or another type for further probing. In the event of a thorough retelling, the comprehension score should be counted independent or instructional, depending upon the accuracy of the retelling and responses to the questions.

An example of a thorough retelling follows. This is John's retelling of Level 2, Form C. (Note the passage found in the Teacher Record on page 105. Also see the Student Record Summary Sheet, page 20, and the Qualitative Analysis Summary Sheet, page 22 for the final writeup of John's reading performance.)

Retelling: This is a story about a dog. The boy in the story yells to his dog, "Look out, you're gonna get hit!" The dog is running across a busy street. The dog gets hit anyway. The boy really feels bad. He almost starts to cry. He runs home to tell his mom and dad that his dog got hit. Someone has to help out.

Examiner
Probe (Mi):   In one or two short sentences, tell me what this story is about.

Student
Response: It's about a dog that got hit in the street.

Examiner
Probe: Do you know the name of the dog?

Student
Response: Shēp (Student miscued the proper noun in the text.)

If a retelling is incomplete, the examiner should probe the reader by saying, "Can you tell me more?" An example of an incomplete retelling follows. This is John's retelling of Level 4, Form C on page 107. See pages 20 and 22 for the final analysis of John's reading performance.

Retelling:	It's about a horse. Joby (word miscued in text) is real worried about the horse. It's sick. The wind blew the barn door open. It started banging.
Examiner Probe:	Can you tell me more?
Student Response:	That night Joby stayed with the horse. The alarm went off and Joby saw some birds. The horse was gone.
Examiner Probe:	Can you tell me more?
Student Response:	No response
Examiner Probe (Mi):	In one or two short sentences, tell what this story is about.
Student Response:	It's about a sick horse. The boy is worried.

When a reader responds to the comprehension questions, he/she may not give the exact response listed as possible answers in the teacher record. The examiner must exercise personal judgment in determining what is an acceptable response. For example, consider the responses to these questions from John's evaluation, Level 4, Form C.

# 3	Why did Jody take a blanket from the house? (so he could sleep near Gabilan)
Student Response:	He wanted to stay all night in the barn with his sick horse.
# 7	How did Jody try to find his pony? (he followed the pony's tracks)
Student Response:	He ran through the banging barn door.
Examiner Probe:	How did Jody know where to look for his pony?
Student Response:	The door was open. The horse was gone.

Even though the response to question #3 is not in the exact words of the suggested response, the examiner determines that John understands why Jody took the blanket to the barn. In question #7, however, even after probing, John really doesn't know that Jody followed the pony's tracks. Examiner judgment, plus additional probing, must be exercised to determine if the student is actually deriving the correct meaning from the text.

Step 5

On the scoring guide at the bottom of the page, circle the appropriate level for both word recognition and comprehension. Sometimes an examiner finds that the miscue count either exceeds or falls short of the range indicated on the scoring guide. In this case a judgment must be made.[4] When determining a student's reading level, keep in mind that comprehension rather than word recognition is the ultimate goal. Some examples based upon the following scoring guide will help to clarify the matter.

Scoring Guide	
Word Rec.	Comp.
Ind 1-2	Ind 0
Inst 7-8	Inst 2
Frust 15+	Frust 4+

If the student made 5 word recognition miscues, produced a thorough retelling, and made zero comprehension mistakes, the level, in most instances, would be determined independent. After a quick assessment to insure that the 5 word recognition miscues have not interfered with comprehension accuracy, the examiner would feel assured of a proper decision. If the student made 7 word recognition miscues, produced an incomplete retelling, and made 7 comprehension mistakes, the level would be frustration. If the student made 10 word recognition miscues, produced a mediocre retelling, and made 3 comprehension mistakes, the level might be low instructional or frustration. A careful look at the severity of the miscues and the overt demeanor of the student would be necessary before a final judgment could be made. If, for example, the word recognition miscues appeared to have little effect on comprehension accuracy and if the student showed no signs of anxiety, then the level would be considered low instructional. However, if there were apparent signs of anxiety during the reading of the passage, and if the miscues severely interfered with comprehension accuracy, then the level would be considered frustration.

If the frustration level has not been reached, have the student read the next passage. After the frustration level has been reached, the student no longer reads. It is then necessary to identify the student's listening level. The listening level is determined by having the examiner read passages to the student. The examiner may choose to read the selection immediately after the passage found to be the reader's frustration level, or choose passages from another form if the examiner wishes to gather information from lower levels.

Step 6

Tell the student that you will read a passage aloud. Ask the student to listen carefully since he will be responsible for retelling the passage and answering some comprehension questions. Stop after the level at which the student comprehends 75% of the material read aloud. On the scoring guide, this is the same as the instructional level.

Step 7

Have the student return to class; then summarize the information discussed in the next section.

Since the successful use of the ARI requires familiarity with informal reading inventory procedures, and since some of the decision making is based upon subjective evaluations, it is recommended that users of this inventory practice its administration sufficiently so that they will thoroughly understand the procedures,

---

[4]This matter is thoroughly discussed in "Informal Reading Inventories: The Instructional Level" by Eldon E. Ekwall from *The Reading Teacher*, April 1976, *29*, 662–65.

the content of the passages, and the nature of the questions before using the inventory.

Summarizing the Results

Several ways of helping the user summarize the results of the student's performance are provided in this inventory. At the bottom of the teacher's copy is a space for tallying the oral reading miscues. There is also a Student Record Summary Sheet on which the results of the diagnosis are to be summarized. This sheet allows for a careful look at the quantitative results of the reading and also provides space for summarizing some qualitative results. Because all deviations from the text are not equally serious, the concern with the quality of the response is important.[5] Following the Student Record Summary Sheet is a Qualitative Analysis Summary Sheet, which some users may find helpful. This sheet allows a closer examination of the student's oral reading and enables the teacher to note if there are possible miscue patterns. The following pages include a sample analysis of the reading behaviors of a student, which should help the examiner to see how a thorough analysis can be derived from the systematic observation of a student's reading patterns. The analysis also includes the subsequent recommendations. These recommendations are intended for use with an individual student and small reading groups, or as suggestions for parents who wish to provide support from the home. All sources for the recommendations are cited in the section of References on page 137 of this inventory. Finally, there is also a Class Record Summary Sheet on page 135 on which the results for 12 students may be summarized. This summary sheet contains spaces for showing the results of three separate administrations of the inventory and may be used to compare beginning-of-year, mid-year, and end-of-year performance.

---

[5]For those who wish a careful treatment of the distinctions between quantitative and qualitative analyses, see Goodman & Burke (1972).

STUDENT RECORD SUMMARY SHEET

Student _John Stone_   Grade _4_   Sex _M_   Age _9 - 10_
                                                      yrs. mos.

School _Merrill Elementary_   Administered by _M. L. Woods_   Date _7/28/86_

Grade	Word Lists	Graded Passages			Estimated Levels	
	% of words correct	WR Form _C_	Comp. Form _C_	Listen. Form _B_		
Primer	100%					
1	100%	⁻¹ Ind.	⁻⁰ Ind.			
2	100%	⁻³ Inst.	⁻² Inst.			Grade
3	95%	⁻⁷ Inst.	⁻³ Inst.	Inst.	Independent	1
4	60%	⁻¹¹ Inst.	⁻⁵ Frust.	Inst.	Instructional	2-3
5		⁻¹⁸ Frust.	⁻⁶ Frust.	Inst.	Frustration	4
6				Frust.	Listening	5
7						
8						
9						

Check consistent oral reading difficulties:

____ word-by-word reading
____ omissions
✓ substitutions ← (makes numerous word guesses)
____ corrections
____ repetitions
____ reversals
✓ inattention to punctuation
____ word inserts
____ requests word help

Check consistent word recognition difficulties:

____ single consonants
____ consonant clusters
✓ long vowels ⎫ medial
✓ short vowels ⎭
____ vowel digraphs
____ diphthongs
____ syllabication
✓ use of context (must strengthen)
____ basic sight
✓ grade level sight

Check consistent comprehension difficulties:

____ main idea
____ factual
✓ terminology
✓ cause and effect
✓ inferential
✓ drawing conclusions
✓ retelling

Description of Reading Behaviors:

   John's oral reading was slow, word-by-word, and laborious. He often ignored the author's punctuation clues, gliding right into the next sentence or phrase.

Word Recognition   He displayed skill in the use of initial consonants and some blends, thus allowing him to pronounce some words. I knew that John was searching for meaning as he read since sometimes he made word substitutions which were appropriate to the meaning of the text. He also self-corrected some miscues, revealing that he was using context clues to recognize words and glean meaning from the text. I was certain that he was, in fact, using context clues since he would return to correct some words after the completion of a sentence or paragraph. Even though John's word recognition instructional level is quantitatively at Level 4, the quality of the miscues revealed more severe difficulties. Since he appears more confident at Levels 2 and 3, the actual instructional level should be stated at Level 3.

Comprehension   The retellings at Levels 2 and 3 contained adequate information about the passages. Level 2 was retold in a manner which followed the author's sequence and logic more so than Level 3. The retelling at Level 4 was organized in a more random manner, never revealing the logic of the passage. After probing from the examiner, John could concisely retell the main idea of Levels 2, 3, and 4.

When he responded to comprehension questions, he consistently recalled factual information more readily than information requiring the reader to correlate portions of the text (Ce questions), or to draw inferences from the text (Inf/Con questions). At Levels 2, 3, and 4 his descriptions of some vocabulary words never adequately revealed their meanings, indicating a weak background vocabulary. When context clues at Levels 2 and 3 were available, the definitions of words became more accurate; however, at Level 4, the ability to use context clues diminished.

Based upon the nature of John's word recognition problems, the disorganization of the retelling, the lack of adequate responses to the comprehension questions, and the physical signs of tiring and stress, it appears as though Level 4 is his frustration level. A quick check done with a reading passage from the fourth grade social studies book revealed the same reading behaviors. A silent reading passage (Level 4) was also given, rendering the same comprehension patterns as found in the oral sample. The miscues at Level 5 were so numerous that comprehension was obliterated.

His listening capacity, Level 5, proved to be above both his instructional and frustration levels. The retelling at Level 4 was better organized and more logical than at Level 5; however, at Level 6, the retelling demonstrated similar organizational patterns found in the oral and silent reading samples at Level 4. This information tells us that John can adequately comprehend slightly more challenging material when he is not confronted with the task of recognizing words in a text. This information should prove useful ·in the selection of material which is read in class, and in determining the complexity of classroom discussions.

Summary of Instructional Level (2–3)

Word Recognition

Confident, self-correcting behavior

Use of initial consonants and some blends

Use of appropriate substitutions

Use of context clues

Comprehension

Adequate retellings following author's logic (more so at Level 2 than 3)

Main idea concisely expressed

Comprehension responses more factual than Cause and Effect or Inferential/Conclusions

Use of context clues to gain meaning of vocabulary

Inadequate descriptions of vocabulary if no context clues are available

Listening Level

Adequate retellings at Levels 4 and 5 (more organized and better use of logic at Level 4 than 5)

QUALITATIVE ANALYSIS SUMMARY SHEET

FORM _C_

Student _John Stone_   Grade ___4___   Sex ___M___   Age _9 – 10_

yrs. mos.

Level	Word in Text	What Child Read	Sampling of Miscues	
			Meaning Change	Nature of Miscue*
2	you'll	you're	✓	final substitution
	lying	down	–	whole word guess – meaning based substitution
	knew	know	✓	medial vowel
	Shep	Shĕp	✓	medial vowel
3	pounding	banging	–	initial/medial guess – meaning based substitution
	declared	remarked	–	initial/medial guess – meaning based substitution
	all	and	✓	sight
	invited	invented	✓	medial vowel
4	Jody	Jŏbe	–	b–d reversal? no significant pattern
	Gabilan	(no attempt)	–	aided word
	even	ever	✓	final substitution
	condition	con/dition	–	vowel mispronunciation
	whipped	blew	✓	whole word guess – meaning based substitution
	awakened	awaked	–	medial omission
5	500	5	✓	final omission
	licensed	listed	✓	medial guess
	most	(omitted)	✓	word omission
	country	county	✓	final omission

Summary and Comments <u>Word Recognition:</u> 1) Substitutions and word guesses (occurring consistently in the medial portion of the word, meaning based substitutions); 2) Grade level sight vocabulary needs strengthening; 3) Use of context clues to recognize words needs strengthening. <u>Comprehension:</u> 1) Inattention to punctuation interfering with comprehension; 2) Retellings poorly organized, esp. at Levels 3 & 4; 3) Vocabulary terms not adequately defined, esp. at Levels 3 & 4; 4) Strategies for cause and effect relationships and drawing inferences need strengthening; 5) Use of context clues needs strengthening.
(See attached recommendations.)

*A miscue may be lack of knowledge of any of the following basic sight words; grade level sight vocabulary; consonant sounds; vowel sounds; blends; digraphs; diphthongs; structural analysis of roots, affixes, possessives, plurals, word families, compound words, accent, and syllabication rules. For complete definitions and suggestions for remediation of each of these miscues, refer to *Locating and Correcting Reading Difficulties*, 4th ed., by Eldon E. Ekwall (Columbus, Ohio: Charles E. Merrill, 1985).

INSTRUCTIONAL RECOMMENDATIONS

Word Recognition

Substitutions, Word Guesses, Context Clues, and
Grade Level Sight Vocabulary

It should be noted that if a reader is to attain comprehension of a particular written context, the vocabulary should always be held in its contextual framework. If word recognition practice is conducted, the isolation of words is not as beneficial to the reader as is recognition in context; therefore, all recommendations which follow should be considered only if the reader is offered the benefit of using the vocabulary in a meaningful context.

1. As the student reads and miscues a word, the teacher, tutor, or parent should provide a synonym or meaning-based phrase for the miscue. The reader should respond with the exact pronunciation of the word, or with a meaningful substitute. This strategy encourages the reader to attend to the meaning of the text, to maintain the flow and pace of the reading, and to maximize the use of context clues.[6]
2. Place sight words, basal vocabulary, and content area vocabulary words on individual cards to be used as study cards. The cards should be kept in a classroom, specific reading group or individual file, and should be continuously updated. Laminate sheets of lined paper (regular or primary). As file words are introduced to or miscued by the reader, the reader should be asked to write (on the laminated sheets with a marker) sentences or mini-stories using the words. The teacher, parent, or tutor should likewise write sentences or mini-stories on their sheet. An example of a sentence and a mini-story is found on p. 25, #10, Context Clues. Sentences and stories can be shared within the group or between individuals. The sheets may then be wiped off, preparing them for reuse. This same strategy can also be done using overhead transparencies, markers, and projector.

---

[6]Adapted from Goodman, Burke, & Sherman (1981), p. 194.

3. Ask questions about the subject matter which will reflect the student's miscue. Have the student find the word in the text and reread the context.
4. Have the reader to reread several words preceding the miscue. The reader should say, "Blank" for the miscued word, then continue onward through the text. This will help the reader to think about the context and to obtain the correct pronunciation for the word.
5. Place an acetate sheet over the reader's text. Have the reader read silently through the text, crossing out selected words in the text with a felt marker. The reader should then read the text aloud to the group or tutor, omitting the crossed-out words. The group or tutor must guess the omitted words by giving the exact word or a meaningful substitution. When the reader is finished, he should remove the sheet, wiping it off for reuse.
6. On laminated lined paper, the chalkboard, or an overhead transparency place the miscued word in a new context. As the teacher, tutor, or parent writes, the reader should simultaneously read along. The reader may recognize the miscue in its new context. The reader should then be encouraged to recognize the miscue in the text.
7. After a text has been completely read, provide review for miscues or words with challenging meanings by:
   a. Placing the word or words in a new context using synonyms.
   Teacher/Tutor/Parent
   writes or says: The boy knew how to *mimic* the comedian, and

   Reader writes
   or says: his brother knew how to *imitate* the same comedian.
   b. Placing the word or words in a new context using antonyms.
   Teacher/Tutor/Parent
   writes or says: The man made an *insignificant* speech, but

   Reader writes
   or says: his opponent's speech was *important.*

Comprehension

Inattention to Punctuation

1. Review the meanings of the various punctuation marks and discuss how they help with proper phrasing and the systematic organization of an author's thoughts. Provide numerous writing experiences so the reader begins to use punctuation marks as a means of making a message clear to another reader. Involvement in the writing process will help the reader to better understand the clues an author uses to convey meaning.

Insufficient Retellings and Improper Sequencing of Events

2. Ask the student to visualize and then verbally describe the events of a reading passage, including all pertinent details. Help the student to organize this description in the appropriate logic by asking such questions as, "What happened first, then second, third, etc?"
3. Place a plastic sheet over a passage which the student has read. Have the student underline and number the events as they occur in the passage with a felt marker. Have the student review the underlined and

numbered portions and verbally describe the passage including all properly sequenced facts.

4. Prior to the reading of the text, have the reader scout through the material, using all pictures, graphics, etc., to gather information. The reader should then be asked to predict the meaning by describing what she thinks will happen in this text.

5. Place an acetate sheet over the beginning portion of the text. Have the reader quickly scout through the material, finding and underlining words which help to reveal its meaning. Have the reader predict the meaning, describing what she thinks will happen in the text. (This could also be done orally by quickly scouting through the material and calling out relevant words or phrases.)

Types of Comprehension Question Weaknesses: Main Idea, Terminology, Cause and Effect Relationships

6. Ask the student or students to read a passage or story, and then write a short gist statement (main idea) on paper. The teacher, tutor, or parent should do the same. Then the statements should be read aloud. After hearing all statements, the most concise, yet thorough one should be discussed. An author may then choose to edit his statement. Edited statements may be kept in a folder and used for rereading and review.

7. Refer to recommendation #2, page 23.

8. Cause and effect (Ce) Explain to the student that cause and effect questions involve a relationship of facts found in a text. Have the student read a passage looking for relationships which tell the cause or effect. The teacher, tutor, or parent should ask the reader questions like: "Why did Sue fall into the river?" (asking for the cause); "What happened after the boy found the 100-dollar bill?" (asking for the effect).
   Find a story which describes the cause of an event. Ask the student to write or tell the ending of the story, producing the effect. Then turn the tables, finding a story which describes the effect, and ask the student to write or tell the ending of the story, producing the cause.

Context Clues

9. Make a tape recording of a passage in which all difficult words are omitted. Give the student a copy of the passage and have him/her fill in the blanks as the tape is played. Accept meaningful substitutions.

10. Add homographs to the vocabulary file. Have the student or students write sentences or mini-stories using them in a context. Have students edit the sentences or stories and place them in a class-made book. Examples might look like the following:
    a. The man held a small lead pipe in his hand. "We will lead our team to victory!" she declared. (sentences)
    b. The bus driver knew that the driving would really be tough. The bus would have to wind around mountainous roads, and the heavy wind would cause the bus to sway back and forth. Despite all of this, he was determined to complete the journey. (mini-story)

FORM A

(Primer)	(1)	(2)
1. not	1. kind	1. mile
2. funny	2. rocket	2. fair
3. book	3. behind	3. ago
4. thank	4. our	4. need
5. good	5. men	5. fourth
6. into	6. met	6. lazy
7. know	7. wish	7. field
8. your	8. told	8. taken
9. come	9. after	9. everything
10. help	10. ready	10. part
11. man	11. barn	11. save
12. now	12. next	12. hide
13. show	13. cat	13. instead
14. want	14. hold	14. bad
15. did	15. story	15. love
16. have	16. turtle	16. breakfast
17. little	17. give	17. reach
18. cake	18. cry	18. song
19. home	19. fight	19. cupcake
20. soon	20. please	20. trunk

(3)

1. beginning
2. thankful
3. written
4. reason
5. bent
6. patient
7. manage
8. arithmetic
9. burst
10. bush
11. gingerbread
12. tremble
13. planet
14. struggle
15. museum
16. grin
17. ill
18. alarm
19. cool
20. engine

(4)

1. worm
2. afford
3. player
4. scientific
5. meek
6. rodeo
7. festival
8. hillside
9. coward
10. boom
11. booth
12. freeze
13. protest
14. nervous
15. sparrow
16. level
17. underground
18. oxen
19. eighty
20. shouldn't

(5)

1. abandon
2. zigzag
3. terrific
4. terrify
5. plantation
6. loaf
7. hike
8. relative
9. available
10. grief
11. physical
12. commander
13. error
14. woodcutter
15. submarine
16. ignore
17. disappointed
18. wrestle
19. vehicle
20. international

(6)

1. seventeen
2. annoy
3. dwindle
4. rival
5. hesitation
6. navigator
7. gorge
8. burglar
9. construction
10. exploration
11. technical
12. spice
13. spike
14. prevail
15. memorial
16. initiation
17. undergrowth
18. ladle
19. walnut
20. tributary

Pat sat by the tree.

"Mom wants me to work," Pat said.

"I do not want to help her work.

I will hide by this big tree.

She will not find me.

I will hide from her.

My mom will not find me.

I will hide by this big tree!"

Terry got into the little car. He had something for Show and Tell in a big paper bag. Next, Bill got into the car with his big paper bag.

Then Ann got into the car. She had something for Show and Tell in a big paper bag, too. Last, Sue got into the car with her paper bag. Now the little car was ready to go to school.

"The little car is getting fat!" said Terry.

The children laughed.

Whiz! The baseball went right by me, and I struck at the air!

"Strike one," called the man. I could feel my legs begin to shake!

Whiz! The ball went by me again, and I began to feel bad. "Strike two," screamed the man.

I held the bat back because this time I would kill the ball! I would hit it right out of the park! I was so scared that I bit down on my lip. My knees shook and my hands grew wet.

Swish! The ball came right over the plate. Crack! I hit it a good one! Then I ran like the wind. Everyone was yelling for me because I was now a baseball star!

The sunlight shined into the mouth of the cave so Mark could see easily at first, but the farther he walked, the darker it grew. Boxer ran off to explore on his own.

Soon it grew so dark Mark could see nothing, but he could hear water dripping off the cave walls. He touched a wall with his hand to find it cold and damp. Mark began to grow fearful, so he lit his candle and held it high to look around.

Suddenly, the flame went out. He heard a low growl near him and saw a pair of fierce, green eyes glowing in the dark! He tried to relight the candle, but the first match went out! Finally, Mark's shaking hand held the lighted candle high.

"Boxer!" he shouted. "Now I recognize those green eyes of yours! Let's get out of here!"

The three were growing tired from their long journey, and now they had to cross a river. It was wide and deep, so they would have to swim across.

The younger dog plunged into the icy water barking for the others to follow him. The older dog jumped into the water. He was weak and suffering from pain, but somehow he managed to struggle to the opposite bank.

The poor cat was left all alone. He was so afraid that he ran up and down the bank wailing with fear. The younger dog swam back and forth trying to help. Finally, the cat jumped and began swimming near his friend.

At that moment something bad happened. An old beaver dam from upstream broke. The water came rushing downstream hurling a large log toward the animals. It struck the cat and swept him helplessly away.

"Look out," Sheila Young thought as she saw her challenger's bicycle come too close. "Watch out, you will foul me!"

At that moment a horrifying thing happened as she was bumped by another racer at forty miles an hour. Sheila's bicycle crashed, and she skidded to the surface of the track. From the wreck she received a nine-inch gash on her head.

The judges ruled that the race should be run again since a foul had been made. Sheila would not have enough time to get her wound stitched. Still, she didn't want to quit the race because she could think only of winning.

"Just staple the cut together with clamps," she told the doctor. "I want to try to win that race!"

The doctor did as Sheila asked. As she stood in silence while being treated, tears rolled down her face from the intense pain. Then, with a blood-stained bandage on her throbbing head, she pushed on to amaze the crowd with a victory and a gold medal!

"Thousands of people are dying on the battlefields from loss of blood," said Dr. Charles Drew. "I must give my time to solving the problems of blood transfusion."

Physicians had studied blood transfusion for years. However, they had met with many difficulties because the whole blood spoiled within days, and the matching of blood types was time-consuming. Nevertheless, Dr. Drew found there were fewer problems if plasma, instead of whole blood, was used in transfusion. Plasma, the liquid part of the blood without the cells, could be stored much longer and made the matching of blood types unnecessary. Anybody could be given plasma, and this was important on the battlefields of World War II.

In 1940 the Blood Transfusion Association set up a program for war-torn France. Dr. Drew asked them to send plasma rather than whole blood. But, it was started too late since France had fallen into the hands of the enemy.

Later, when Great Britain suffered heavy losses from air raids, Dr. Drew was asked to run a program called "Plasma for Britain." He organized the entire project, and thousands of Americans gave blood to help the British.

While he had been hiding out for the past five days, Johnny had given serious thought to the whole mess. He had decided to return home, turn himself in to the police, and take the consequences of his crime. Being only sixteen, he was too young to have to run away for the rest of his life. He knew the fight had been in self-defense, but the fact still remained that he had killed another person, and the thought of that miserable night in the city park sent Johnny into a terrifying panic.

He told Dally and Ponyboy of his decision, and now Dally reluctantly began the long drive home. Dally had gone to jail before, and this was one wretched experience he did not want his friend to have to endure.

As they reached the top of Jay Mountain, Dally slammed on the brakes! The old church where Johnny and Ponyboy had been hiding was in flames! Ponyboy and Johnny bolted from the car to question a bystander who explained that they were having a school picnic when the church began to burn.

Suddenly, the crowd was shocked to hear desperate cries from inside! Ponyboy and Johnny ran into the burning church, and the boys lifted the children one by one through a window to safety. Chunks of the old roof were already beginning to fall as the last child was taken out. Ponyboy leaped through the window, vaguely hearing the sound of falling timber. Then, as he lay coughing and exhausted on the ground, he heard Johnny's terrifying scream!

Witch-hunts were common in seventeenth-century England. The mere presence of a witch-hunter in a village caused such fear among the people that children would even denounce their parents.

Belief in magic was common in those days. Perhaps some of the victims of these hunts did think themselves guilty of witchery, but history has proven that the majority of men and women accused and tortured by witch-hunters were but poor, defenseless victims of the times.

One of the best-known methods for the detection of a witch was the "swimming test." In this ordeal the suspect was dragged into a pool or stream after he was already tired from torture and fear. If the suspect floated to the top he was found guilty, and long pins were plunged into his body in search of the devil's marks. If he sank to the bottom, he was presumed innocent.

In 1645 a man who titled himself Witchfinder General Matthew Hopkins led a severe and cruel hunt. Because a civil war was raging in England at the time, tensions and fears were common among the people. The time was ripe for persecution.

In that same year Hopkins imprisoned as many as 200 persons, all charged with witchcraft. Among eighteen of those who died by hanging was one John Lowes, a seventy-year-old clergyman who had been accused of witchcraft by his congregation. After undergoing intolerable torture, the old man admitted ownership of an evil spirit which he allegedly ordered to sink a ship. No one bothered to check out the existence of such a vessel or to ask about any reported sinkings on that day, and he was hanged after reading his own burial service.

"This lake is all treated sewer water," the old gentleman murmured in admiration. The old man sat on a bench as close to the bank as possible with his elbows resting on his knees while gazing at the rippling water. The breeze sweeping across the lake caused the sailboats to glide about with amazing ease.

"We are making great ecological strides," he thought to himself. He knew well the story of this remarkable lake nestled in the foothills of southern California. He swelled with pride to recall the wise choice the Santee citizens had made when they elected not to join the metropolitan sewage system where the waste would have been discharged into the Pacific with only inadequate primary treatment. Rather, the residents constructed their own sewage facility, reclaiming the sewer water, thus extending their own supply to provide basic needs and clean recreational extras.

"This is probably the only city park in the world which is built just yards downstream from a sewer plant," the gentleman thought. He leaned forward scooping up a handful of water. "This lake is more sanitary than most natural streams."

It had taken ingenious foresight to make this unprecedented plan viable. Its resourcefulness lay in the fact that clean water provided not only lucrative recreational facilities, but the sewage waste solids furnished marketable soil conditioners and plant fertilizers.

As the old gentleman arose he caught sight of paper trash carelessly tossed beside the shore. His contented expression changed to one of concern. He already knew that twenty million tons of paper are discarded each year in the United States representing a net loss of 340 million trees to the environment. The gentleman shook his head to think of this needless waste. He knew the United States comprises only 6 percent of the world's population, yet its citizens consume 30 percent of the world's total energy output, only to waste half of it. The old gentleman shuddered at these thoughts as he picked up the discarded paper and placed it into the trash container.

FORM A

Teacher Record

STUDENT RECORD SUMMARY SHEET

Student _____ Grade _____ Sex _____ Age _____
yrs. mos.

School _____ Administered by _____ Date _____

Grade	Word Lists	Graded Passages			Estimated Levels		
	% of words correct	WR Form ____	Comp. Form ____	Listen. Form ____			
Primer							
1							
2						Independent	Grade _____
3						Instructional	_____
4						Frustration	_____
5						Listening	_____
6							
7							
8							
9							

Check consistent oral reading difficulties:

____ word-by-word reading

____ omissions

____ substitutions

____ corrections

____ repetitions

____ reversals

____ inattention to punctuation

____ word inserts

____ requests word help

Check consistent word recognition difficulties:

____ single consonants

____ consonant clusters

____ long vowels

____ short vowels

____ vowel digraphs

____ diphthongs

____ syllabication

____ use of context

____ basic sight

____ grade level sight

Check consistent comprehension difficulties:

____ main idea

____ factual

____ terminology

____ cause and effect

____ inferential

____ drawing conclusions

____ retelling

Description of reading behaviors:

_____

_____

_____

_____

QUALITATIVE ANALYSIS SUMMARY SHEET

FORM _____

Student _____ Grade _____ Sex _____ Age _____
                                                                      yrs. mos.

Level	Word in Text	What Child Read	Sampling of Miscues	
			Meaning Change	Nature of Miscue*

Summary Comments _____
_____
_____
_____
_____
_____
_____

*A miscue may be lack of knowledge of any of the following: basic sight words; grade level sight vocabulary; consonant sounds; vowel sounds; blends; digraphs; diphthongs; structural analysis of roots, affixes, possessives, plurals, word families, compound words, accent, and syllabication rules. For complete definitions and suggestions for remediation of each of these miscues, refer to Ekwall (1985).

(Student Booklet page 28)

(Primer)	(1)	(2)
1. not _____	1. kind _____	1. mile _____
2. funny _____	2. rocket _____	2. fair _____
3. book _____	3. behind _____	3. ago _____
4. thank _____	4. our _____	4. need _____
5. good _____	5. men _____	5. fourth _____
6. into _____	6. met _____	6. lazy _____
7. know _____	7. wish _____	7. field _____
8. your _____	8. told _____	8. taken _____
9. come _____	9. after _____	9. everything _____
10. help _____	10. ready _____	10. part _____
11. man _____	11. barn _____	11. save _____
12. now _____	12. next _____	12. hide _____
13. show _____	13. cat _____	13. instead _____
14. want _____	14. hold _____	14. bad _____
15. did _____	15. story _____	15. love _____
16. have _____	16. turtle _____	16. breakfast _____
17. little _____	17. give _____	17. reach _____
18. cake _____	18. cry _____	18. song _____
19. home _____	19. fight _____	19. cupcake _____
20. soon _____	20. please _____	20. trunk _____

(Student Booklet page 29)

(3)

1. beginning_____
2. thankful_____
3. written_____
4. reason_____
5. bent_____
6. patient_____
7. manage_____
8. arithmetic_____
9. burst_____
10. bush_____
11. gingerbread_____
12. tremble_____
13. planet_____
14. struggle_____
15. museum_____
16. grin_____
17. ill_____
18. alarm_____
19. cool_____
20. engine_____

(4)

1. worm_____
2. afford_____
3. player_____
4. scientific_____
5. meek_____
6. rodeo_____
7. festival_____
8. hillside_____
9. coward_____
10. boom_____
11. booth_____
12. freeze_____
13. protest_____
14. nervous_____
15. sparrow_____
16. level_____
17. underground_____
18. oxen_____
19. eighty_____
20. shouldn't_____

(5)

1. abandon_____
2. zigzag_____
3. terrific_____
4. terrify_____
5. plantation_____
6. loaf_____
7. hike_____
8. relative_____
9. available_____
10. grief_____
11. physical_____
12. commander_____
13. error_____
14. woodcutter_____
15. submarine_____
16. ignore_____
17. disappointed_____
18. wrestle_____
19. vehicle_____
20. international_____

(6)

1. seventeen_____
2. annoy_____
3. dwindle_____
4. rival_____
5. hesitation_____
6. navigator_____
7. gorge_____
8. burglar_____
9. construction_____
10. exploration_____
11. technical_____
12. spice_____
13. spike_____
14. prevail_____
15. memorial_____
16. initiation_____
17. undergrowth_____
18. ladle_____
19. walnut_____
20. tributary_____

Primer (50 words   8 sent.)

Examiner's Introduction (Student Booklet page 31): Pat is thinking about fooling Mom. Have you ever thought about tricking your folks? Please read about Pat.

Pat sat by the tree.

"Mom wants me to work," Pat said.

"I do not want to help her work.

I will hide by this big tree.

She will not find me.

I will hide from her.

My mom will not find me.

I will hide by this big tree!"

Comprehension Questions and Possible Answers

(mi) 1. What is this story about?
(Hiding from mom, getting out of work, etc.)

(f) 2. Where is Pat sitting?
(by the big tree)

(t) 3. What does the word *work* mean in this story?
(to do a chore or to do something you are supposed to do)

(ce) 4. Why is Pat going to hide by the big tree?
(so Pat's mom will not find Pat)

(f) 5. What does Pat's mom want Pat to do?
(help her work)

(inf) 6. What is said in the story which makes you think Pat doesn't want to work?
(Stated: I don't want to help her work, so I'll hide from her.)

Miscue Count:

O___ I___ S___ A___ REP___ REV___

Scoring Guide		
Word Rec.		Comp.
IND	0–1	IND	0
INST	2–3	INST	1–2
FRUST 5+		FRUST 3+

**Examiner's Introduction
(Student Booklet page 32):** In this story the young children are being picked up for school. Please read about this special day.

Terry got into the little car. He had something for Show and Tell in a big paper bag. Next, Bill got into the car with his big paper bag.

Then Ann got into the car. She had something for Show and Tell in a big paper bag, too. Last, Sue got into the car with her paper bag. Now the little car was ready to go to school.

''The little car is getting fat!'' said Terry.

The children laughed.

**Comprehension Questions
and Possible Answers**

(mi) 1. What is this story about?
(The day for Show and Tell, going to school for Show and Tell, etc.)

(f) 2. How did the children carry their things to school?
(in paper bags)

(ce) 3. What happened after the last child got into the car?
(The little car was ready to go to school.)

(f) 4. What did the children do when Terry said, ''The little car is getting fat''?
(They laughed.)

(t) 5. In this story what does the word *ready* mean?
(all set to go to school or the car was full)

(inf) 6. What did Terry mean when he said that he thought the little car was getting fat?
(The car was getting crowded.)

Miscue Count:

O____I____S____A____REP____REV____

Scoring Guide	
Word Rec.	Comp.
IND 0–1	IND 0
INST 3–4	INST 1–2
FRUST 8 +	FRUST 3 +

Level 2 (118 words   13 sent.)

Examiner's Introduction (Student Booklet page 33): Imagine how you would feel if you were up to bat and this was your team's last chance to win the game! Please read this story.

Whiz! The baseball went right by me, and I struck at the air!

"Strike one," called the man. I could feel my legs begin to shake!

Whiz! The ball went by me again, and I began to feel bad. "Strike two," screamed the man.

I held the bat back because this time I would kill the ball! I would hit it right out of the park! I was so scared that I bit down on my lip. My knees shook and my hands grew wet.

Swish! The ball came right over the plate. Crack! I hit it a good one! Then I ran like the wind. Everyone was yelling for me because I was now a baseball star!

Comprehension Questions and Possible Answers

(mi) 1. What is this story about?
(a baseball game, someone who gets two strikes and finally gets a hit, etc.)

(f) 2. After the second strike, what did the batter plan to do?
(hit the ball right out of the park)

(inf) 3. Who was the "man" in this story who called the strikes?
(the umpire)

(t) 4. In this story, what was meant when the batter said, "I would kill the ball"?
(hit it very hard)

(ce) 5. Why was the last pitch a good one?
(because it went right over the plate)

(ce) 6. What did the batter do after the last pitch?
(The batter hit it a good one and ran like the wind.)

Miscue Count:

O____ I____ S____ A____ REP____ REV____

Scoring Guide	
Word Rec.	Comp.
IND 1	IND 0
INST 6	INST 1–2
FRUST 12+	FRUST 3+

Level 3 (143 words 12 sent.)

Mark's dad had warned him not to go near the cave, but Mark and his dog, Boxer, had ideas of their own. Please read this story.

The sunlight shined into the mouth of the cave so Mark could see easily at first, but the farther he walked, the darker it grew. Boxer ran off to explore on his own.

Soon it grew so dark Mark could see nothing, but he could hear water dripping off the cave walls. He touched a wall with his hand to find it cold and damp. Mark began to grow fearful, so he lit his candle and held it high to look around.

Suddenly, the flame went out. He heard a low growl near him and saw a pair of fierce, green eyes glowing in the dark! He tried to relight the candle, but the first match went out! Finally, Mark's shaking hand held the lighted candle high.

"Boxer!" he shouted. "Now I recognize those green eyes of yours! Let's get out of here!"

Comprehension Questions and Possible Answers

(mi) 1. In this story what were Mark and Boxer doing?
(exploring a cave)

(f) 2. In what part of the cave was the sunlight?
(the mouth of the cave)

(f) 3. When they first entered the cave, what did Boxer do?
(ran off to explore on his own)

(t) 4. What is meant by the word *farther*?
(Mark went a greater distance into the cave.)

(t) 5. What is meant by the word *recognize*?
(to see something that you know)

(ce) 6. Why did Mark light the candle the first time?
(It grew dark and he got scared.)

(inf) 7. What makes you think Mark was scared when the candle went out?
(He tried to relight the candle and his hand shook.)

(f) 8. What were the low growl and the fierce, green eyes?
(his dog, Boxer)

Miscue Count:

O____ I____ S____ A____ REP____ REV____

Scoring Guide		
Word Rec.		Comp.
IND	1–2	IND	0
INST	7–8	INST	2
FRUST	15+	FRUST	4+

Level 4 (144 words 13 sent.)

Examiner's Introduction (Student Booklet page 35): If you like excitement then you will enjoy reading the *Incredible Journey* by Sheila Burnford. This story is about three pets, a cat and two dogs, whose owners leave the animals when they move to another country. The animals decide to try to find their owners but face many hardships. Please read a retelling of one of the incidents from this exciting story.

The three were growing tired from their long journey, and now they had to cross a river. It was wide and deep, so they would have to swim across.

The younger dog plunged into the icy water, barking for the others to follow him. The older dog jumped into the water. He was weak and suffering from pain, but somehow he managed to struggle to the opposite bank.

The poor cat was left all alone. He was so afraid that he ran up and down the bank wailing with fear. The younger dog swam back and forth trying to help. Finally, the cat jumped and began swimming near his friend.

At that moment something bad happened. An old beaver dam from upstream broke. The water came rushing downstream hurling a large log toward the animals. It struck the cat and swept him helplessly away.

Comprehension Questions and Possible Answers

(mi) 1. In this passage what was the difficult thing the animals had to do?
(cross a river)

(f) 2. How would the animals get across the river?
(They would have to swim.)

(t) 3. What is the meaning of *plunged*?
(to jump in quickly)

(ce) 4. Why did the younger dog bark at the other animals?
(to try to get them to follow him)

(f) 5. What is meant by the phrase "wailing with fear"?
(to be so scared that one cries out)

(f) 6. After the cat jumped in, what bad thing happened?
(An old beaver dam broke.)

(ce) 7. Why did the log come hurling downstream?
(The rushing water brought it.)

(con) 8. What makes you think the animals were run down and in poor health?
(Stated: They were tired; the old dog was suffering from pain.)

Miscue Count:

O____ I____ S____ A____ REP____ REV____

Scoring Guide		
Word Rec.		Comp.
IND	1–2	IND	0–1
INST	7–8	INST	2
FRUST 15+		FRUST 4+

Form A / Teacher Record / Graded Paragraphs

**Examiner's Introduction
(Student Booklet page 36):**

Sheila Young enjoys bicycling and once competed in World and Olympic championship races. Please read about something that happened to Sheila during a cycling race. This passage is based upon information from an article entitled, "Sportswomanlike Conduct," appearing in a 1974 issue of *Newsweek*.

"Look out," Sheila Young thought as she saw her challenger's bicycle come too close. "Watch out, you will foul me!"

At that moment a horrifying thing happened as she was bumped by another racer at forty miles an hour. Sheila's bicycle crashed, and she skidded to the surface of the track. From the wreck she received a nine-inch gash on her head.

The judges ruled that the race should be run again since a foul had been made. Sheila would not have enough time to get her wound stitched. Still, she didn't want to quit the race because she could think only of winning.

"Just staple the cut together with clamps," she told the doctor. "I want to try to win that race!"

The doctor did as Sheila asked. As she stood in silence while being treated, tears rolled down her face from the intense pain. Then, with a blood-stained bandage on her throbbing head, she pushed on to amaze the crowd with a victory and a gold medal!

**Comprehension Questions
and Possible Answers**

(mi) 1. In this passage, what horrifying thing happened to Sheila Young?
(She was fouled, causing a wreck and injury.)

(t)   2. What is a "challenger"?
(someone who says they can beat you in competition; another competitor)

(f)   3. What injury did Sheila receive in the wreck?
(a nine-inch gash on her head)

(ce) 4. In this passage, why didn't she want to quit the race?
(She could think only of winning.)

(f)   5. What did she ask the doctor to do for her?
(staple the cut with a clamp)

(t)   6. What is meant by the phrase "intense pain"?
(strong pain)

(ce) 7. Why did tears run down Sheila's face?
(As she was being treated, her wound was painful.)

(con) 8. What is said in the story that makes you think this race was an important one?
(Stated: Even though she had been hurt, the judges could not delay the race for her sake;
the prize was a gold medal.)

Miscue Count:

O____ I____ S____ A____ REP____ REV____

Scoring Guide	
Word Rec.	Comp.
IND 2	IND 0–1
INST 9	INST 2
FRUST 18+	FRUST 4+

Examiner's Introduction
(Student Booklet page 37):
Dr. Charles Drew overcame many obstacles to become a remarkable black American surgeon. Dr. Drew, who died in an auto crash at the age of forty-six, lived a life of dedication and kindness. The following information was derived from a book entitled, *Black Pioneers of Science and Invention*, by Louis Haber.

"Thousands of people are dying on the battlefields from loss of blood," said Dr. Charles Drew. "I must give my time to solving the problems of blood transfusion."

Physicians had studied blood transfusion for years. However, they had met with many difficulties because the whole blood spoiled within days, and the matching of blood types was time-consuming. Nevertheless, Dr. Drew found there were fewer problems if plasma, instead of whole blood, was used in transfusion. Plasma, the liquid part of the blood without the cells, could be stored much longer and made the matching of blood types unnecessary. Anybody could be given plasma, and this was important on the battlefields of World War II.

In 1940 the Blood Transfusion Association set up a program for war-torn France. Dr. Drew asked them to send plasma rather than whole blood. But it was started too late since France had fallen into the hands of the enemy.

Later, when Great Britain suffered heavy losses from air raids, Dr. Drew was asked to run a program called "Plasma for Britain." He organized the entire project, and thousands of Americans gave blood to help the British.

**Comprehension Questions
and Possible Answers**

(mi) 1. What was the area of Dr. Drew's major work?
(blood transfusion)

(t) 2. What is meant by the word *difficulties*?
(problems)

(ce) 3. Why did Dr. Drew decide to devote his time to solving the problems of blood transfusion?
(Thousands were dying on the battlefields of World War II.)

(f)   4. What is plasma?
(the liquid portion of the blood without cells)

(ce)   5. Why is plasma so useful?
(it can be stored much longer than whole blood or it made the matching of blood types unnecessary)

(f)   6. What is meant by the phrase, ''fallen into the hands of the enemy''?
(France had been defeated or taken over by the enemy.)

(ce)   7. Why did Americans give blood to help their British neighbors?
(Britain had suffered heavy losses from air raids.)

(con)   8. What is said in this story that makes you think more people survived injuries on the battle-field because of Dr. Drew's work in blood transfusion?
(Stated: Plasma could be stored longer; with plasma, blood typing was unnecessary; anybody could be given plasma.)

Miscue Count:

O____ I____ S____ A____ REP____ REV____

Scoring Guide		
Word Rec.		Comp.
IND	2	IND 0–1
INST	10	INST 2
FRUST	20+	FRUST 4+

Examiner's Introduction (Student Booklet page 38): S. E. Hinton wrote a very sensitive book called *The Outsiders*, showing the loyalties teen-agers in gangs have toward one another. In this passage, Johnny is in serious trouble, and his friends, Ponyboy and Dally, prefer to stick by him until he can decide how best to solve his problem. Please read a retelling of one of the incidents from this memorable book.

While he had been hiding out for the past five days, Johnny had given serious thought to the whole mess. He had decided to return home, turn himself in to the police, and take the consequences of his crime. Being only sixteen, he was too young to have to run away for the rest of his life. He knew the fight had been in self-defense, but the fact still remained that he had killed another person, and the thought of that miserable night in the city park sent Johnny into a terrifying panic.

He told Dally and Ponyboy of his decision, and now Dally reluctantly began the long drive home. Dally had gone to jail before, and this was one wretched experience he did not want his friend to have to endure.

As they reached the top of Jay Mountain, Dally slammed on the brakes! The old church where Johnny and Ponyboy had been hiding was in flames! Ponyboy and Johnny bolted from the car to question a bystander who explained that they were having a school picnic when the church began to burn.

Suddenly, the crowd was shocked to hear desperate cries from inside! Ponyboy and Johnny ran into the burning church, and the boys lifted the children one by one through a window to safety. Chunks of the old roof were already beginning to fall as the last child was taken out. Ponyboy leaped through the window, vaguely hearing the sound of falling timber. Then, as he lay coughing and exhausted on the ground, he heard Johnny's terrifying scream!

Comprehension Questions and Possible Answers

(mi)   1. What difficult conflict did Johnny have to solve?
(He had committed a crime, and he had to decide whether to turn himself in to the police or to run away.)

(t)   2. What is meant by the phrase, "take the consequences"?
(take the punishment for his crime)

(f)   3. Where did the crime take place?
(in the city park)

(ce)   4. Why were Dally and the boys returning home?
(Johnny had decided to return home and turn himself in.)

(ce)   5. Why did Dally slam on the brakes?
(He saw the burning church.)

(f)   6. How did the boys get the childern out of the burning church?
(lifted them through the window)

(t)   7. What is meant by the word *vaguely*?
(not clearly defined, unclear)

(con)   8. What is said in the story that makes you think Johnny thought he should turn himself in?
(Stated: He said that he was too young to run and hide for the rest of his life; the fact still remained that he had killed another person, and this was apparently something he felt he couldn't live with.)

Miscue Count:

O____ I____ S____ A____ REP____ REV____

Scoring Guide	
Word Rec.	Comp.
IND 2–3	IND 0–1
INST 13	INST 2
FRUST 26+	FRUST 4+

**Examiner's Introduction
(Student Booklet page 39):**

Witch-hunts took place in England back in the 1600s. The following information was derived from an article entitled, "East Anglican and Essex Witches," from *Man, Myth, and Magic: An Illustrated Encyclopedia of the Supernatural.*

Witch-hunts were common in seventeenth-century England. The mere presence of a witch-hunter in a village caused such fear among the people that children would even denounce their parents.

Belief in magic was common in those days. Perhaps some of the victims of these hunts did think themselves guilty of witchery, but history has proven that the majority of men and women accused and tortured by witch-hunters were but poor, defenseless victims of the times.

One of the best-known methods for the detection of a witch was the "swimming test." In this ordeal the suspect was dragged into a pool or stream after he was already tired from torture and fear. If the suspect floated to the top he was found guilty, and long pins were plunged into his body in search of the devil's marks. If he sank to the bottom, he was presumed innocent.

In 1645 a man who titled himself Witchfinder General Matthew Hopkins led a severe and cruel hunt. Because a civil war was raging in England at the time, tensions and fears were common among the people. The time was ripe for persecution.

In that same year Hopkins imprisoned as many as 200 persons, all charged with witchcraft. Among eighteen of those who died by hanging was one John Lowes, a seventy-year-old clergyman who had been accused of witchcraft by his congregation. After undergoing intolerable torture, the old man admitted ownership of an evil spirit which he allegedly ordered to sink a ship. No one bothered to check out the existence of such a vessel or to ask about any reported sinkings on that day, and he was hanged after reading his own burial service.

**Comprehension Questions
and Possible Answers**

(mi)   1. What commonly happened in seventeenth-century England?
(witch-hunts)

(f)   2. According to this passage, what has history proven about witch-hunts?
(Most of the men and women accused and tortured for being witches were but poor and defenseless people.)

(ce) 3. Why would children even denounce their parents as witches?
      (The mere presence of a witch-finder caused such fear among the people and children.)

(t)   4. What is meant by the phrase, "method of detection"?
      (way of finding something out)

(ce) 5. In seventeenth-century England, why was the time ripe for persecution?
      (A civil war was raging, causing tension and fear.)

(t)   6. What is meant by the word *allegedly*?
      (asserted to be true or exist but not proven)

(f)   7. What did John Lowes allegedly do?
      (owned an evil spirit which sank a ship)

(inf) 8. What is said in the story that makes you think the swimming test was unjust?
      (Stated: If the accused person sank, thus being proven innocent, he or she was probably dead from drowning.)

Miscue Count:

O____ I____ S____ A____ REP____ REV____

Scoring Guide		
Word Rec.		Comp.
IND	3	IND	0–1
INST	15	INST	2
FRUST	30+	FRUST	4+

**Examiner's Introduction
(Student Booklet page 40):**

This selection, based upon information from two articles appearing in a 1973 issue of *Plain Truth*, entitled, "Who's That Polluting My World?" and "How One Town Solves Pollution and Saves Water," describes some interesting facts concerning pollution and its control.

"This lake is all treated sewer water," the old gentleman murmured in admiration. The old man sat on a bench as close to the bank as possible with his elbows resting on his knees while gazing at the rippling water. The breeze sweeping across the lake caused the sailboats to glide about with amazing ease.

"We are making great ecological strides," he thought to himself. He knew well the story of this remarkable lake nestled in the foothills of southern California. He swelled with pride to recall the wise choice the Santee citizens had made when they elected not to join the metropolitan sewage system where the waste would have been discharged into the Pacific with only inadequate primary treatment. Rather, the residents constructed their own sewage facility, reclaiming the sewer water, thus extending their own supply to provide basic needs and clean recreational extras.

"This is probably the only city park in the world which is built just yards downstream from a sewer plant," the gentleman thought. He leaned forward scooping up a handful of water. "This lake is more sanitary than most natural streams."

It had taken ingenious foresight to make this unprecedented plan viable. Its resourcefulness lay in the fact that clean water provided not only lucrative recreational facilities, but the sewage waste solids furnished marketable soil conditioners and plant fertilizers.

As the old gentleman arose he caught sight of paper trash carelessly tossed beside the shore. His contented expression changed to one of concern. He already knew that twenty million tons of paper are discarded each year in the United States representing a net loss of 340 million trees to the environment. The gentleman shook his head to think of this needless waste. He knew the United States comprises only 6 percent of the world's population, yet its citizens consume 30 percent of the world's total energy output, only to waste half of it. The old gentleman shuddered at these thoughts as he picked up the discarded paper and placed it into the trash container.

Comprehension Questions and Possible Answers

(mi) 1. What is the main idea of this passage?
(We are making progress in pollution control, but still there is needless waste.)

(t) 2. What is meant by the phrase *inadequate primary treatment*?
(insufficient water treatment)

(f) 3. Where is this remarkable lake?
(in Santee in southern California)

(ce) 4. What happened when the Santee citizens constructed their own sewage facility?
(It provided basic needs and clean recreational extras.)

(t) 5. What is meant by the phrase *an unprecedented plan*?
(one not done before)

(f) 6. How much of the world's total energy does the United States use?
(30 percent)

(ce) 7. Why did the old gentleman's expression change when he got up from the bench?
(He caught sight of paper trash carelessly tossed beside the shore.)

(inf) 8. What is said in the story that makes you think that the plan to reclaim the sewage water was ingenious and well thought-out?
(Stated: The clean water provided not only lucrative recreational facilities, but the waste solids furnished marketable soil conditioners and plant fertilizers.)

Miscue Count:

O____ I____ S____ A____ REP____ REV____

Scoring Guide		
Word Rec.	Comp.	
IND 3–4	IND 0–1	
INST 18	INST 2	
FRUST 36+	FRUST 4+	

Form A / Teacher Record / Graded Paragraphs

FORM B

	(Primer)		(1)		(2)
1.	birthday	1.	town	1.	yet
2.	went	2.	bear	2.	minute
3.	fish	3.	sound	3.	act
4.	like	4.	party	4.	bunny
5.	something	5.	there	5.	empty
6.	blue	6.	these	6.	inside
7.	that	7.	don't	7.	squirrel
8.	they	8.	brown	8.	thumb
9.	train	9.	shoe	9.	grandmother
10.	what	10.	light	10.	dragon
11.	mother	11.	hair	11.	elephant
12.	ride	12.	water	12.	I'd
13.	house	13.	own	13.	threw
14.	new	14.	race	14.	beautiful
15.	here	15.	why	15.	roof
16.	paint	16.	hear	16.	through
17.	work	17.	fly	17.	leave
18.	stop	18.	grass	18.	unhappy
19.	away	19.	morning	19.	garden
20.	around	20.	animal	20.	branch

(3)

1. broom
2. hammer
3. log
4. step
5. question
6. wrinkle
7. invisible
8. vegetable
9. engineer
10. allow
11. knee
12. excitement
13. storm
14. repair
15. sweep
16. swept
17. million
18. buzz
19. doorbell
20. you've

(4)

1. zebra
2. liberty
3. mend
4. dolphin
5. ability
6. compound
7. gentlemen
8. holly
9. swamp
10. swarm
11. chill
12. wreck
13. solid
14. alphabet
15. holiday
16. equal
17. dull
18. shiver
19. they're
20. nonsense

1. splendor
2. mason
3. radiant
4. cease
5. fisherman
6. brief
7. distress
8. fake
9. false
10. gust
11. proceed
12. triumph
13. scuffle
14. operation
15. military
16. hull
17. genius
18. contribution
19. reverse
20. indicate

1. counterclockwise
2. diesel
3. mathematical
4. representative
5. accomplishment
6. extraordinary
7. congratulation
8. daily
9. odor
10. resemble
11. acquire
12. combine
13. opportunity
14. transparent
15. transport
16. cheap
17. fifteenth
18. phase
19. violet
20. woolen

"I will grow tall," said Sally.
"I will grow tall like my mom.
I will grow tall fast.
My face will grow too.
I know my nose will grow.
What if my nose does not grow?
Then my nose will be a little baby nose!
I will look very funny!"

"Hurry," said Sue Brown. "Hide the balloons, and then all of us hide! Hurry, but don't make a sound or say a word! I see Dad coming up the walk now!"

When Father came into the house he didn't see his children. All was still and he could hear nothing.

Then Father did hear and see something. He heard his children laughing, singing, and calling "Surprise!" He saw fat blue and green balloons flying in the air!

Swish! My pet mouse ran straight under our neighbor's chair! Our neighbor didn't hear him because he is quiet, as a mouse should be. If she had seen him she would have yelled her head off.

Zoom! Now my clever gray mouse is bouncing off the jam jar on the breakfast table. He is sliding on the milk left around my glass! He is dancing on my cupcake!

He loves drinking lemonade. He eats lots of honey and blueberries. He is silly, different, and really quite funny. I'll always love my dear little mouse.

Say, have you seen my sweet gray friend? You better look now because he is right under your chair!

Joe sat down on the sidewalk in front of the trading post with his buckskin jacket thrown over his shoulder. He felt worried because it was difficult to know what to do.

"Grandfather told me never to sell these blue beads. He said they would bring me good fortune and good health. Grandfather is a wise and understanding man. He is proud to be an American Indian. He remembers when his grandfather gave him these same beads. He has often told me many interesting stories of how his grandfather rode horses and hunted buffalo on the plains."

Joe held the string of beads high into the air toward the sunlight. "These are perfectly beautiful beads," he said out loud. "I can't sell them because I too am proud of my great past. Yes, I will keep the beads!"

Joel's Pa was storming mad! Joel Goss had journeyed far with the schoolmaster to help him collect some money, and now they had returned not with money but with two colts! His father was furious.

The news had spread throughout the county that one of the colts was very small, and people had already begun to laugh. Joel had hoped to calm his father's anger by convincing him of Little Bub's strength, but Mr. Goss was still raging with anger! He pounded his fist on the table shouting several commands! The schoolmaster must find another place to live! The colts could not stay on the property!

Then he turned to Joel. It was time that Joel leave his house and find a job. In the morning they would visit Miller Chase and ask him to take Joel to work in the sawmill. Joel felt shocked and hurt! How could he leave his own home and Little Bub?

"I know that I was last in the race," announced Robyn Smith, "but I am determined to be the best woman jockey! I want to ride race horses!"

It was a rainy morning in 1969, and as Robyn stood outside talking to the trainer, Frank Wright, she was so dripping wet that water came running out of the top of her boots. Many people had doubts about Robyn's riding ability, but Wright was sure she could be a successful rider. He decided to give her a first big chance.

By December of that same year she had proven herself by placing fourth in a race. Robyn not only had skill as a jockey, but she also had a way with horses which made them run fast for her.

Soon she became accepted by others as an excellent rider. She went on to highlight her career with a surprising victory riding a horse named North Star. This horse was known for being wild on the track, but Robyn was able to handle him. Together they outran a horse named Onion. This was a special victory for Robyn because later, in another race, Onion defeated the famous horse, Secretariat!

The explosion was horrible that tragic day in Cleveland, Ohio, in 1916. Thirty-two men were trapped in a tunnel 250 feet below Lake Erie. No one could enter the smoke-filled tunnel to rescue the survivors.

"Someone get Garrett Morgan to help those men down there," shouted a man from the crowd. "Morgan and his breathing device are the only chance those men have!"

Garrett Morgan and his brother quickly came to the aid of the men trapped in the tunnel. Morgan had invented what he called a "Breathing Device," later to be known as the gas mask. Two years before, Morgan's invention had been tested by filling an enclosed tent with the foulest, thickest smoke possible. Placing the device over his head, a man entered this suffocating atmosphere, stayed twenty minutes, and emerged unharmed! Later, using a poisonous gas in a closed room, another test also provided the same successful results.

Although not all lived, every man was brought to the surface by the brothers. It was Morgan's concern for safer working conditions that saved lives that day and in the years to come.

Kate sat in her senior biology class, but she wasn't hearing a single word the teacher was saying since her mind was thoroughly preoccupied. She could only think about Dave and her date with him last Friday night.

The entire thing was so confusing and distracting that she kept glancing sideways to where he was sitting near the windows. He was by far the most handsome boy at Tylerton High. He was tall, strong, with shaggy hair, and brilliant blue eyes, but there was something very different about Dave Burdick which she found difficult to accept. She knew that he was independent, and at times he seemed actually defiant. She found this disturbing. He always neglected his appearance as if he didn't care what others thought. He was an excellent football player, probably the best in the entire school, but he quit the team. He was stubborn and belligerent, and he would argue with anyone over anything. He never hung around the other kids, so it seemed to her that he was a loner. He drove an old Ford pickup, which had chicken feathers and farm tools scattered all over the floor. Kate felt that he was more interested in raising chickens than in having friends. Yet, even knowing all of these things, there was something crazy going on in her mind. To her surprise she found Dave Burdick fascinating and quite to her liking.

You've probably said something like this yourself, "I was so exhausted I was a walking zombie!" On the island of Haiti in the Caribbean Sea, belief in zombies and the supernatural is common.

A *zombie* is characterized as a resurrected body brought back to half-life by magic. A zombie walks with a faltering gait, keeps downcast eyes, speaks garbled words, if it speaks at all, and generally displays abnormal behavior.

Some stories have actually been written describing zombies. For example, there is one depicting a girl who was allegedly discovered working in a small shop four years after her death. Even though this story was published, it has not been definitely verified.

A magistrate from Haiti once told a convincing tale about a man who went blind after seeing a troupe of zombies marching in the hills. It was his feeling that this was no laughing matter. Then he went on to tell his own eyewitness yarn of a body which arose from its grave as a half-alive figure and walked about the graveyard. Of course he continued to tell that this was an enormous hoax. The following day, he examined the grave to find a pipe leading from it to the fresh air where the imposter could breathe!

Supposedly, zombies can be owned by a living person. It is said if zombies are given something salty to eat or drink they will awaken from their trance. Thus, another tale has been told about a man whose wife mistakenly fed his zombies some salted biscuits. Awakened from their trance, these zombies hurried off to the cemetery, hurled themselves upon their graves, and attempted to dig themselves back into the earth.

As the Michaud family entered the village of Shimshal, the villagers abandoned their work and ran to welcome the travelers. They were the first Europeans the people of Shimshal had seen in twenty-seven years!

Shimshal, situated at an altitude of 10,000 feet, is the most remote village in Hunza. Located near a junction between China, the Soviet Union, Afghanistan, Pakistan and India, Hunza rests among the steep towers and deep gorges of the mountains.

The Michauds' journey took place in the spring of the year, so the danger of avalanches was always present. To reach Shimshal the party picked their way along the mountain ledges with painstaking care. Along the arduous trail lay several obstacles. For example, a suspension bridge consisting of stretched cables for handrails and planks for a footpath provided the only way to cross a dangerous river.

Shimshal has 5,000 to 6,000 inhabitants. Despite the fact that by Western standards these people are quite poor, the Michauds found them to be most generous and hospitable. They are a solid people living a life consisting of vigorous physical exercise, an adequate nutritional diet, and freedom from emotional stress. It is purported that many of them live to be as old as a century or more, thus attracting the attention of the outside world. Studies have been done to analyze the life-style of the Hunzakuts in an attempt to understand the secrets of longevity.

Their diet, consisting primarily of whole grains and fresh fruits, is of particular interest to the outside world. Because fuel is scarce, the food is minimally cooked and therefore maintains most of its nutritional value. Meat is rarely included in the diet because of limited pasture land. The Hunzakuts' steady nature is often attributed to dietary habits. At the turn of the century, a famous physician of British India wrote: "Their nerves are as solid as cables and sensitive as the strings of a violin."

FORM B

Teacher Record

STUDENT RECORD SUMMARY SHEET

Student _____ Grade _____ Sex _____ Age _____
yrs. mos.

School _____ Administered by _____ Date _____

Grade	Word Lists	Graded Passages			Estimated Levels		
	% of words correct	WR Form ____	Comp. Form ____	Listen. Form ____			
Primer							
1							
2						Grade	
3					Independent	_____	
4					Instructional	_____	
5					Frustration	_____	
6					Listening	_____	
7							
8							
9							

Check consistent oral reading difficulties:

____ word-by-word reading
____ omissions
____ substitutions
____ corrections
____ repetitions
____ reversals
____ inattention to punctuation
____ word inserts
____ requests word help

Check consistent word recognition difficulties:

____ single consonants
____ consonant clusters
____ long vowels
____ short vowels
____ vowel digraphs
____ diphthongs
____ syllabication
____ use of context
____ basic sight
____ grade level sight

Check consistent comprehension difficulties:

____ main idea
____ factual
____ terminology
____ cause and effect
____ inferential
____ drawing conclusions
____ retelling

Description of Reading Behaviors:

_____

_____

_____

_____

QUALITATIVE ANALYSIS SUMMARY SHEET

FORM _____

Student _____ Grade _____ Sex _____ Age _____
yrs. mos.

Level	Word in Text	What Child Read	Sampling of Miscues	
			Meaning Change	Nature of Miscue*

Summary and Comments _____

_____

_____

_____

_____

_____

*A miscue may be lack of knowledge of any of the following: basic sight words; grade level sight vocabulary; consonant sounds; vowel sounds; blends; digraphs; diphthongs; structural analysis of roots, affixes, possessives, plurals, word families, compound words, accent, and syllabication rules. For complete definitions and suggestions for remediation of each of these miscues, refer to Ekwall (1985).

(Student Booklet page 64)

(Primer)	(1)	(2)
1. birthday_____	1. town_____	1. yet_____
2. went_____	2. bear_____	2. minute_____
3. fish_____	3. sound_____	3. act_____
4. like_____	4. party_____	4. bunny_____
5. something_____	5. there_____	5. empty_____
6. blue_____	6. these_____	6. inside_____
7. that_____	7. don't_____	7. squirrel_____
8. they_____	8. brown_____	8. thumb_____
9. train_____	9. shoe_____	9. grandmother_____
10. what_____	10. light_____	10. dragon_____
11. mother_____	11. hair_____	11. elephant_____
12. ride_____	12. water_____	12. I'd_____
13. house_____	13. own_____	13. threw_____
14. new_____	14. race_____	14. beautiful_____
15. here_____	15. why_____	15. roof_____
16. paint_____	16. hear_____	16. through_____
17. work_____	17. fly_____	17. leave_____
18. stop_____	18. grass_____	18. unhappy_____
19. away_____	19. morning_____	19. garden_____
20. around_____	20. animal_____	20. branch_____

(Student Booklet page 65)

(3)

1. broom_____
2. hammer_____
3. log_____
4. step_____
5. question_____
6. wrinkle_____
7. invisible_____
8. vegetable_____
9. engineer_____
10. allow_____
11. knee_____
12. excitement_____
13. storm_____
14. repair_____
15. sweep_____
16. swept_____
17. million_____
18. buzz_____
19. doorbell_____
20. you've_____

(4)

1. zebra_____
2. liberty_____
3. mend_____
4. dolphin_____
5. ability_____
6. compound_____
7. gentlemen_____
8. holly_____
9. swamp_____
10. swarm_____
11. chill_____
12. wreck_____
13. solid_____
14. alphabet_____
15. holiday_____
16. equal_____
17. dull_____
18. shiver_____
19. they're_____
20. nonsense_____

(Student Booklet page 66)

(5)

1. splendor _____
2. mason _____
3. radiant _____
4. cease _____
5. fisherman _____
6. brief _____
7. distress _____
8. fake _____
9. false _____
10. gust _____
11. proceed _____
12. triumph _____
13. scuffle _____
14. operation _____
15. military _____
16. hull _____
17. genius _____
18. contribution _____
19. reverse _____
20. indicate _____

(6)

1. counterclockwise _____
2. diesel _____
3. mathematical _____
4. representative _____
5. accomplishment _____
6. extraordinary _____
7. congratulation _____
8. daily _____
9. odor _____
10. resemble _____
11. acquire _____
12. combine _____
13. opportunity _____
14. transparent _____
15. transport _____
16. cheap _____
17. fifteenth _____
18. phase _____
19. violet _____
20. woolen _____

Primer (50 words   8 sent.)

**Examiner's Introduction
(Student Booklet page 67):** Sally is looking at herself in the mirror and has a silly thought about herself. Please read to see what she is thinking.

"I will grow tall," said Sally.

"I will grow tall like my mom.

I will grow tall fast.

My face will grow too.

I know my nose will grow.

What if my nose does not grow?

Then my nose will be a little baby nose!

I will look very funny!"

**Comprehension Questions
and Possible Answers**

(mi)   1. What is this story about?
(Sally grows tall, growing with a funny nose, etc.)

(f)   2. How does Sally think she will grow?
(tall, fast, like her mom)

(t)   3. In this story what does *funny* mean?
(odd, different, strange, possibly silly)

(t)   4. What does the word *grow* mean?
(to get bigger)

(ce)   5. What will happen if Sally's nose does not grow?
(She will have a baby nose.)

(inf)   6. Do you think Sally really believes that her nose will stay a baby nose?
(No, she says that she knows her nose will grow.)

Miscue Count:

O____ I____ S____ A____ REP____ REV____

Scoring Guide	
Word Rec.	Comp.
IND 0–1	IND 0
INST 2–3	INST 1–2
FRUST 5+	FRUST 3+

**Examiner's Introduction
(Student Booklet page 68):**   We all like special parties. You will now read about one given for someone very special.

"Hurry," said Sue Brown. "Hide the balloons,
and then all of us hide! Hurry, but don't make a
sound or say a word! I see Dad coming up the walk
now!"

When Father came into the house he didn't
see his children. All was still and he could hear
nothing.

Then Father did hear and see something. He
heard his children laughing, singing, and calling
"Surprise!" He saw fat blue and green balloons
flying in the air!

**Comprehension Questions
and Possible Answers**

(mi)   1. What is this story about?
(A surprise for Dad, a party for Dad, etc.)

(ce)   2. Why did Sue hurry to hide the balloons?
(Because Father was coming up the walk.)

(t)   3. In this story what is meant by the word walk?
(a concrete sidewalk)

(f)   4. What color balloons were flying in the air?
(blue and green)

(ce)   5. What did the children do after Father was in the house?
(The children laughed, sang, and called "Surprise!")

(con) 6. What is said in the story that makes you think the children were going to surprise
their father?
(Stated: All was still; he couldn't see or hear anything.)

Miscue Count:

O_____ I_____ S_____ A_____ REP_____ REV_____

Scoring Guide		
Word Rec.		Comp.
IND	0–1	IND 0
INST	3–4	INST 1–2
FRUST	8+	FRUST 3+

Examiner's Introduction
(Student Booklet page 69):   You are about to read of a very special and rather extraordinary animal.

Swish! My pet mouse ran straight under our neighbor's chair! Our neighbor didn't hear him because he is quiet, as a mouse should be. If she had seen him she would have yelled her head off.

Zoom! Now my clever gray mouse is bouncing off the jam jar on the breakfast table. He is sliding on the milk left around my glass! He is dancing on my cupcake!

He loves drinking lemonade. He eats lots of honey and blueberries. He is silly, different, and really quite funny. I'll always love my dear little mouse.

Say, have you seen my sweet gray friend? You better look now because he is right under your chair!

Comprehension Questions
and Possible Answers

(mi) 1. What is a good title for this story?
("My Pet Mouse")

(f)   2. What color is this mouse?
(gray)

(t)   3. In this story, what is meant by *clever*?
(skillful, quick, smart)

(f)   4. What does this unusual mouse like to drink?
(lemonade)

(ce) 5. Why didn't the neighbor see or hear the mouse?
(The mouse is quiet, as a mouse should be.)

(con) 6. What is said in the story that makes you think that people might be scared of a mouse?
(Stated: The neighbor would have yelled her head off; you'd better look out because the mouse is under your chair!)

Miscue Count:

O____ I____ S____ A____ REP____ REV____

Scoring Guide		
Word Rec.		Comp.
IND	1	IND	0
INST	6	INST	1–2
FRUST	12+	FRUST	3+

**Examiner's Introduction
(Student Booklet page 70):**

Joe wanted more than anything in the world to buy the electric train set in the trading post window. But should he do this? Please read the following story.

Joe sat down on the sidewalk in front of the trading post with his buckskin jacket thrown over his shoulder. He felt worried because it was difficult to know what to do.

"Grandfather told me never to sell these blue beads. He said they would bring me good fortune and good health. Grandfather is a wise and understanding man. He is proud to be an American Indian. He remembers when his grandfather gave him these same beads. He has often told me many interesting stories of how his grandfather rode horses and hunted buffalo on the plains."

Joe held the string of beads high into the air toward the sunlight. "These are perfectly beautiful beads," he said out loud. "I can't sell them because I too am proud of my great past. Yes, I will keep the beads!"

**Comprehension Questions
and Possible Answers**

(mi) 1. What is Joe's difficult decision?
(whether to sell the beads his grandfather had given him)

(f) 2. Where was Joe sitting?
(on the sidewalk in front of the trading post)

(f) 3. What did Joe's grandfather say the beads would do for Joe?
(bring him good fortune and good health)

(t) 4. What is meant by the word *remembers*?
(to recall from the past)

(f) 5. Who had given the beads to Joe's grandfather?
(Joe's great-great grandfather or Joe's grandfather's grandfather)

(t) 6. In the phrase "hunted buffalo on the plains", what is meant by "on the plains"?
(western great plains or large, flat country land)

(ce) 7. Why did Joe finally decide he couldn't sell the beads?
(He was proud of his past.)

(con) 8. What is said in the story that makes you think Joe has respect for his grandfather?
(Stated: Grandfather is a wise and understanding man; he couldn't sell the beads.)

Miscue Count:

O____ I____ S____ A____ REP____ REV____

	Scoring Guide	
Word Rec.		Comp.
IND 1–2		IND 0–1
INST 7		INST 2
FRUST 14+		FRUST 4+

Form B / Teacher Record / Graded Paragraphs

Level 4 (157 words   13 sent.)

Examiner's Introduction (Student Booklet page 71):

Justin Morgan Had A Horse, written by Marguerite Henry, is the thrilling story, set in colonial days, of a small runt work colt who grew to be the father of the famous American Morgan horses. Please read a retelling of one of the incidents from this exciting story.

Joel's Pa was storming mad! Joel Goss had journeyed far with the schoolmaster to help him collect some money, and now they had returned not with money but with two colts! His father was furious.

The news had spread throughout the county that one of the colts was very small, and people had already begun to laugh. Joel had hoped to calm his father's anger by convincing him of Little Bub's strength, but Mr. Goss was still raging with anger! He pounded his fist on the table shouting several commands! The schoolmaster must find another place to live! The colts could not stay on the property!

Then he turned to Joel. It was time that Joel leave his house and find a job. In the morning they would visit Miller Chase and ask him to take Joel to work in the sawmill. Joel felt shocked and hurt! How could he leave his own home and Little Bub?

Comprehension Questions and Possible Answers

(mi)   1. In this story, why was Joel's father so angry?
(Joel and the schoolmaster had not returned from their journey with money, but rather with two unwanted colts.)

(t)   2. What is meant by the word *furious*?
(very mad or angry)

(ce)   3. Why had people begun to laugh about one of the colts?
(One of the colts was very small.)

(t)   4. What is meant by the word *commands* in the phrase "shouting several commands"?
(to give orders or to direct someone)

(f)   5. How had Joel hoped to calm his father's anger?
(by convincing him of Little Bub's strength)

(f)   6. What did Mr. Goss tell the schoolmaster he must do?
(find another place to live)

(f)   7. What did Mr. Goss tell Joel he must do?
(leave his house and find a job)

(inf)   8. What makes you think Joel was upset by what his father said to him?
(Stated: He felt shocked and hurt.)

Miscue Count:

O___ I___ S___ A___ REP___ REV___

Scoring Guide			
Word Rec.		Comp.	
IND	1–2	IND	0–1
INST	7–8	INST	2
FRUST	15+	FRUST	4+

Examiner's Introduction (Student Booklet page 72): This is a story about Robyn Smith who left a career as a movie star to become one of the first female jockeys. The following information was derived from an article appearing in *The Lincoln Library of Sports Champions.*

"I know that I was last in the race," announced Robyn Smith, "but I am determined to be the best woman jockey! I want to ride race horses!"

It was a rainy morning in 1969, and as Robyn stood outside talking to the trainer, Frank Wright, she was so dripping wet that water came running out of the top of her boots. Many people had doubts about Robyn's riding ability, but Wright was sure she could be a successful rider. He decided to give her a first big chance.

By December of that same year she had proven herself by placing fourth in a race. Robyn not only had skill as a jockey, but she also had a way with horses which made them run fast for her.

Soon she became accepted by others as an excellent rider. She went on to highlight her career with a surprising victory riding a horse named North Star. This horse was known for being wild on the track, but Robyn was able to handle him. Together they outran a horse named Onion. This was a special victory for Robyn because later, in another race, Onion defeated the famous horse, Secretariat!

Comprehension Questions and Possible Answers

(mi) 1. What was Robyn Smith determined to be?
(the best woman jockey)

(ce) 2. Why did water run out of the top of Robyn's boots?
(because she was standing outside in the rain)

(f) 3. What did Frank Wright do for Robyn?
(gave her a first big chance)

(t) 4. What is meant by the phrase, "proven herself"?
(She showed that she could ride well.)

(f) 5. What did others think of Robyn when she proved her riding skill?
(She was accepted as a good jockey.)

6. What was the horse she rode known for?
   (being wild on the track)

7. Why was this a special victory for Robyn?
   (North Star defeated Onion; Onion defeated the famous horse Secretariat.)

8. Why do you think Robyn's trainer had confidence in her riding?
   (Stated: Wright was sure she could be a successful rider; she had a way with horses which made them run fast for her; she had skill as a rider.)

Miscue Count:

O____ I____ S____ A____ REP____ REV____

Scoring Guide		
Word Rec.		Comp.
IND	2	IND	0–1
INST	9	INST	2
FRUST	18+	FRUST	4+

**Examiner's Introduction
(Student Booklet page 73):**

Garrett A. Morgan, a black American inventor, was born in 1877. He not only invented the first electric traffic signal but also other important inventions. The following information was derived from a book entitled, *Black Pioneers of Science and Invention*, by Louis Haber.

The explosion was horrible that tragic day in Cleveland, Ohio, in 1916. Thirty-two men were trapped in a tunnel 250 feet below Lake Erie. No one could enter the smoke-filled tunnel to rescue the survivors.

"Someone get Garrett Morgan to help those men down there," shouted a man from the crowd. "Morgan and his breathing device are the only chance those men have!"

Garrett Morgan and his brother quickly came to the aid of the men trapped in the tunnel. Morgan had invented what he called a "Breathing Device," later to be known as the *gas mask*. Two years before, Morgan's invention had been tested by filling an enclosed tent with the foulest, thickest smoke possible. Placing the device over his head, a man entered this suffocating atmosphere, stayed twenty minutes, and emerged unharmed! Later, using a poisonous gas in a closed room, another test also provided the same successful results.

Although not all lived, every man was brought to the surface by the brothers. It was Morgan's concern for safer working conditions that saved lives that day and in the years to come.

**Comprehension Questions
and Possible Answers**

(mi) 1. What did Garrett Morgan invent?
(gas mask—breathing device)

(f) 2. Where was the tunnel located in which the men were trapped?
(250 feet below Lake Erie)

(ce) 3. What happened as a result of the terrible explosion in Cleveland?
(thirty-two men were trapped)

(t) 4. What is meant by the phrase, "this suffocating atmosphere"?
(the air in the tent was without oxygen)

(t) 5. What is meant by the word *device*?
(something intricate in design; a machine)

(ce) 6. What happened to the man who stayed in the tent for twenty minutes?
(He emerged unharmed.)

(f)   7. What was used to test the gas mask the second time?
       (a poisonous gas)

(inf)   8. What is said in the story that makes you think Morgan cared for the safety of others?
       (Stated: It was Morgan's concern for safer working conditions which saved lives that day.)

Miscue Count:

O____ I____ S____ A____ REP____ REV____

Scoring Guide	
Word Rec.	Comp.
IND 2	IND 0–1
INST 10	INST 2
FRUST 20+	FRUST 4+

**Examiner's Introduction
(Student Booklet page 74):**

Dave's Song, a book by Robert McKay, is a sensitive story about a girl who finds out that she can care for someone quite different from her other friends. Please read a retelling of part of this book.

Kate sat in her senior biology class, but she wasn't hearing a single word the teacher was saying since her mind was thoroughly preoccupied. She could only think about Dave and her date with him last Friday night.

The entire thing was so confusing and distracting that she kept glancing sideways to where he was sitting near the windows. He was by far the most handsome boy at Tylerton High. He was tall, strong, with shaggy hair, and brilliant blue eyes, but there was something very different about Dave Burdick which she found difficult to accept. She knew that he was independent, and at times he seemed actually defiant. She found this disturbing. He always neglected his appearance as if he didn't care what others thought. He was an excellent football player, probably the best in the entire school, but he quit the team. He was stubborn and belligerent, and he would argue with anyone over anything. He never hung around the other kids, so it seemed to her that he was a loner. He drove an old Ford pickup, which had chicken feathers and farm tools scattered all over the floor. Kate felt that he was more interested in raising chickens than in having friends. Yet, even knowing all of these things, there was something crazy going on in her mind. To her surprise she found Dave Burdick fascinating and quite to her liking.

**Comprehension Questions
and Possible Answers**

(mi)   1. Why was Kate confused and distracted?
(Dave was very different from her other friends, but she still found that she liked him.)

(ce)   2. Why didn't Kate hear anything the biology teacher was saying?
(She was preoccupied.)

(t)   3. What is meant by the word *independent*?
(not dependent upon others)

(f)   4. What did Kate find disturbing about Dave?
(his defiant attitude)

(t)   5. What is meant by the word *belligerent*?
(hostile, waging war)

(f)   6. What did Dave's truck have in it?
(chicken feathers and old farm tools)

(ce)   7. Why did Kate think Dave was a loner?
       (because he never hung around other kids)

(inf) 8. What is said in the story that makes you think Dave had a negative attitude?
       (Stated: He seemed defiant, stubborn, belligerent.)

Miscue Count:

O____ I____ S____ A____ REP____ REV____

Scoring Guide		
Word Rec.		Comp.
IND 2–3		IND 0–1
INST 13		INST 2
FRUST 26+		FRUST 4+

Level 8 (281 words   16 sent.)

**Examiner's Introduction
(Student Booklet page 75):** The next selection is about zombies. Some people believe in them and some say there is a logical explanation for would-be zombies. The following information was derived from an article entitled, "Zombies," from *Man, Myth, and Magic: An Illustrated Encyclopedia of the Supernatural.*

You've probably said something like this yourself, "I was so exhausted I was a walking zombie!" On the island of Haiti in the Caribbean Sea, belief in zombies and the supernatural is common.

A *zombie* is characterized as a resurrected body brought back to half-life by magic. A zombie walks with a faltering gait, keeps downcast eyes, speaks garbled words, if it speaks at all, and generally displays abnormal behavior.

Some stories have actually been written describing zombies. For example, there is one depicting a girl who was allegedly discovered working in a small shop four years after her death. Even though this story was published, it has not been definitely verified.

A magistrate from Haiti once told a convincing tale about a man who went blind after seeing a troupe of zombies marching in the hills. It was his feeling that this was no laughing matter. Then he went on to tell his own eyewitness yarn of a body which arose from its grave as a half-alive figure and walked about the graveyard. Of course he continued to tell that this was an enormous hoax. The following day, he examined the grave to find a pipe leading from it to the fresh air where the imposter could breathe!

Supposedly, zombies can be owned by a living person. It is said if zombies are given something salty to eat or drink they will awaken from their trance. Thus, another tale has been told about a man whose wife mistakenly fed his zombies some salted biscuits. Awakened from their trance, these zombies hurried off to the cemetery, hurled themselves upon their graves, and attempted to dig themselves back into the earth.

**Comprehension Questions
and Possible Answers**

(mi) 1. What is an unusual belief which exists in Haiti?
      (belief in zombies, or the supernatural)

(t)   2. How does this passage define a *zombie*?
      (a resurrected body brought back to half-life)

Form B / Teacher Record / Graded Paragraphs

(f) 3. Where is Haiti located?
     (in the Caribbean Sea)

(f) 4. How long after her alleged death had the girl been found working in the small shop?
     (four years)

(t) 5. What is meant by the word *hoax*?
     (a trick causing deception)

(ce) 6. Why was the imposter able to breathe?
     (He had a pipe under the grave leading to the fresh air.)

(ce) 7. What happened when the man's wife fed the zombies salty biscuits?
     (They awakened from their trance, hurried off to the cemetery and tried to bury themselves
     in their graves.)

(inf) 8. What is said that makes you think the magistrate took the tale about the zombies in
      the hills seriously?
      (Stated: He said that it was no laughing matter.)

Miscue Count:

O____ I____ S____ A____ REP____ REV____

Scoring Guide			
Word Rec.		Comp.	
IND	3	IND	0–1
INST	15	INST	2
FRUST	30+	FRUST	4+

**Examiner's Introduction
(Student Booklet page 76):**

In this story, a European family visits an isolated area in Asia called Hunza to study ancient traditions. They learned, however, that to find real traditions they must hike the dangerous mountain trails to Shimshal in Upper Hunza. This selection is based upon information taken from an article which appeared in *National Geographic.*

As the Michaud family entered the village of Shimshal, the villagers abandoned their work and ran to welcome the travelers. They were the first Europeans the people of Shimshal had seen in twenty-seven years!

Shimshal, situated at an altitude of 10,000 feet, is the most remote village in Hunza. Located near a junction between China, the Soviet Union, Afghanistan, Pakistan and India, Hunza rests among the steep towers and deep gorges of the mountains.

The Michauds' journey took place in the spring of the year, so the danger of avalanches was always present. To reach Shimshal the party picked their way along the mountain ledges with painstaking care. Along the arduous trail lay several obstacles. For example, a suspension bridge consisting of stretched cables for handrails and planks for a footpath provided the only way to cross a dangerous river.

Shimshal has 5,000 to 6,000 inhabitants. Despite the fact that by Western standards these people are quite poor, the Michauds found them to be most generous and hospitable. They are a solid people living a life consisting of vigorous physical exercise, an adequate nutritional diet, and freedom from emotional stress. It is purported that many of them live to be as old as a century or more, thus attracting the attention of the outside world. Studies have been done to analyze the life-style of the Hunzakuts in an attempt to understand the secrets of longevity.

Their diet, consisting primarily of whole grains and fresh fruits, is of particular interest to the outside world. Because fuel is scarce, the food is minimally cooked and therefore maintains most of its nutritional value. Meat is rarely included in the diet because of limited pasture land. The Hunzakuts' steady nature is often attributed to

Level 9 (continued)

dietary habits. At the turn of the century, a famous physician of British India wrote:

"Their nerves are as solid as cables and sensitive as the strings of a violin."

Comprehension Questions and Possible Answers

(mi) 1. What is the main idea of this article?
(The Michaud family visited a remote village in Hunza, bringing knowledge of this land's traditions to the Western world.)

(f) 2. Where is Shimshal located?
(at an altitude of 10,000 feet in the land of Hunza)

(t) 3. What is meant by the word *arduous*?
(hard to accomplish or achieve)

(f) 4. Despite the fact that the people are poor, what is their disposition like?
(generous and hospitable)

(t) 5. What is meant by the phrase, *"freedom from emotional stress"*?
(their society is free from mental tension)

(ce) 6. Why have studies been done on the life-style of the Hunzakuts?
(in an attempt to understand the secrets of longevity)

(ce) 7. Why is their food minimally cooked?
(fuel is so scarce)

(con) 8. What is said in the story that makes you think the Hunzakuts are good-natured people?
(Stated: They are generous and hospitable; they are a solid yet sensitive people; they have a steady nature.)

Miscue Count:

O____ I____ S____ A____ REP____ REV____

Scoring Guide			
Word Rec.		Comp.	
IND	3–4	IND	0–1
INST	18	INST	2
FRUST	36+	FRUST	4+

FORM C

Student Booklet

(Primer)	(1)	(2)
1. about	1. ice	1. goose
2. can	2. before	2. mouse
3. who	3. another	3. library
4. with	4. children	4. teacher
5. some	5. stopped	5. kite
6. goat	6. hurry	6. cart
7. out	7. drop	7. different
8. trees	8. friend	8. anyone
9. father	9. balloon	9. feather
10. red	10. when	10. pie
11. green	11. where	11. sidewalk
12. make	12. those	12. straight
13. is	13. picnic	13. telephone
14. yes	14. laugh	14. clean
15. saw	15. farm	15. remember
16. get	16. airplane	16. wood
17. ball	17. tomorrow	17. summer
18. and	18. wagon	18. bell
19. down	19. made	19. gun
20. are	20. surprise	20. matter

(3)

1. clap
2. fright
3. diamond
4. silence
5. nurse
6. wiggle
7. precious
8. salt
9. bread
10. breath
11. fellow
12. several
13. unusual
14. overhead
15. driven
16. fool
17. darkness
18. honor
19. screen
20. they'll

(4)

1. canoe
2. hasn't
3. dozen
4. motion
5. pride
6. vicious
7. concern
8. harvest
9. sample
10. official
11. windshield
12. human
13. humor
14. decorate
15. slender
16. seventh
17. parachute
18. good-bye
19. dignity
20. trudge

(5)

1. prevent
2. kindle
3. grease
4. typical
5. foam
6. blur
7. mumps
8. telegram
9. vision
10. sandal
11. argument
12. hail
13. halt
14. region
15. manager
16. sleet
17. yarn
18. parallel
19. coconut
20. dissolve

(6)

1. midstream
2. lens
3. bail
4. college
5. failure
6. falter
7. width
8. graceful
9. somewhat
10. privacy
11. microphone
12. particle
13. clutter
14. applaud
15. vapor
16. reluctant
17. contract
18. nephew
19. insurance
20. fund

Look! It is me!
I can run as fast as a train!
I can jump over a big tall tree!
I can ride my bike as fast as a running goat!
I can see very little things far away.
I can put on a good show!
Yes, I am something!

I found a lost baby turtle. I took him home so he could live in my house. A friend gave me his prize rabbit. I took the rabbit home to live in my house.

I found a lost duck so I took her home too. I saw a little, cold blackbird and took him home. Then, I saw a cow who looked so sad. I took her home!

But Mom said, "No! No! Not a cow!"

"Look out, you'll get hit!" I yelled as Shep ran across the busy road. "Thud!" was the noise I heard, and then I saw my pup lying in the street. "Oh, no!" I shouted. I felt scared inside.

"Shep is my best friend!" I wanted to cry out. I knew that he was hurt, but he'd be all right if I could get help fast. I knew I had to be brave.

"Mom! Dad!" I yelled as I ran straight home. I tried to fight back the tears. But they started rolling down my face anyway as I blasted through the door. "Shep has been hit, and he's badly hurt!" I cried out. "Please hurry and help him!"

FOR NEIGHBORHOOD TIGERS ONLY! KNOCK ONE THOUSAND TIMES AND SAY THE SECRET WORD BEFORE ENTERING!

These were the signs which Jack read as he stood outside the neighborhood clubhouse. Jack was a new boy, and he really wanted to belong to the club. "How can I get the kids to agree to let me belong?" he thought. Suddenly he dashed home and soon returned with a bucket of yellow paint, one of black, and several brushes. He began pounding on the clubhouse door.

"I'm knocking a thousand times!" he shouted. "I don't know the secret word," he declared, "but I have something important to tell everyone! I'm the new boy," he explained. "Since the name of your club is 'Tigers,' I thought you might want to paint your clubhouse yellow with black stripes!"

All the kids thought this was a great idea and quickly invited Jack to belong!

Jody was so worried that he didn't even care to eat. He had stayed in the barn all day to take care of his sick pony, Gabilan. The pony's condition was growing worse as his breathing grew louder and harder.

At nightfall Jody brought a blanket from the house so he could sleep near Gabilan. In the middle of the night a wind whipped around the barn and blew the door open.

At dawn Jody awakened to the banging of the barn door. Gabilan was gone! In alarm he ran from the barn following the pony's tracks. Looking upward he saw buzzards, the birds of death, flying overhead. Jody stood still, then ran to the top of a small hill. In a clearing below, he saw something that filled his heart with anger and hate. A buzzard was perched on his dying pony's head.

"I want to be the fastest woman driver in the world," stated Shirley Muldowney. "I'd really like to go 500 miles per hour, but I'll be happy to go 400 this year and try for 500 next year," she quickly added.

Shirley, nicknamed Cha Cha, is presently the only woman licensed to drive Top Fuel cars. These cars are the fastest, the most powerful, and among the most carefully built machines in the car racing sport. Not only is she licensed to drive Top Fuel cars, but she is now one of the top challengers in the country. She has established a top speed of 241.58 miles per hour. No Top Fuel driver has reached a speed of over 250 miles per hour.

Shirley has a great deal of energy, determination, and nerve. She is confident that she can drive her car to victory. It is characteristic of her to accomplish about anything she sets out to do. A good friend has said, "It's been a long time since people thought of her just as a woman who drives race cars. She's a top driver who just happens to be a woman!"

James Cornish lay wounded on the saloon floor! "He's been stabbed in the chest!" shouted one horrified bystander. "Someone get him to a hospital!" another shouted.

It was a hot and humid day in Chicago in 1893. Cornish arrived at the hospital with a one-inch knife wound in his chest, dangerously near his heart. Dr. Daniel Hale Williams was called in to operate.

In those days when blood transfusions and antibiotics were unknown, chest surgery was rarely attempted since it meant a high risk of death. As Dr. Williams began to operate, he found that the stab wound had cut the heart and the sac around the heart. Dr. Williams then made history by becoming the first surgeon to successfully operate on the human heart.

Dr. Williams did not release this information for three and a half years. When he did, the newspaper headline read, "Sewed Up His Heart," and the news became known to the entire world. Not only had Cornish been discharged from the hospital a well man, but he lived fifty years after his surgery. Cornish even outlived the surgeon who had saved his life.

Jim was sixteen years old, and he thought more of his older brother, Kevin, than anyone else. He had informed all his friends that he'd not see them during the summer because he would be spending all his time with Kevin. It would be a terrific summer because Kevin was the greatest guy in the world.

But when Kevin arrived home from his first year at college something was different about him; he seemed unsettled, stayed confined to his room, and requested that Jim not disturb him. He wasn't interested in talking over old times. In fact, everything seemed to bore him.

Soon Jim discovered that Kevin had changed. Kevin smoked grass and spent his days beating the streets looking for LSD. Jim was stunned, bewildered, and to make things worse, it seemed to him that their parents didn't notice any unusual change in Kevin's personality.

Then one evening that inevitable occurrence which goes along with the drug scene happened. Kevin had taken the LSD near the time their folks left the house. It wasn't long before Jim found his brother convulsing, writhing on the floor, hallucinating, and unconsciously screaming out crazy things.

It was a frightful experience for Jim to see Kevin in such torture. He was terrorized with fear as he hurled himself on top of Kevin, grabbing at his arms in an attempt to keep his brother from injuring himself. He knew he had to get help immediately!

"I am . . . Dracula," murmured a black-caped, fanged-toothed, pointed-eared monster. "I never drink . . . wine," he declared as movie-goers sat petrified in their seats.

In 1931, a novel by Irish author Bram Stoker became vividly alive on the movie screen as thousands flocked to see this re-creation of the vampire superstition which dates back to the sixteenth century.

According to the novel, a vampire looks pale, lean, and has a death-like icy touch. His eyes gleam or flash red, his ears are pointed like those of a werewolf, and his fingernails are curled and sharp. Some tales describe him as skeletal and often dressed in a black costume. His limited diet of blood gives him a foul-smelling breath. Old legends depict him with only one nostril and a barbed tongue. These creatures have the power to change their form into a cloud of mist or a bizarre nocturnal animal.

Despite modern disbelief in vampires, during the seventeenth century many thought they existed. It was believed that once a person died he could possibly return as a vampire. A corpse was often fastened in its grave with pegs or iron skewers to prevent a potential vampire from escaping.

Since the vampire was dormant during the day, graves were examined for small holes through which the monster could escape. If a grave was discovered with such holes, vampire hunters would remove the body and destroy it. This procedure took place during the daytime hours and all the hunters returned to their homes before sunset.

A young Pygmy stood in the parching equatorial African sun. He stood but five feet tall and his stature was bent from hard labor. His skin was golden brown and his hair was short and curled tightly to his head. His feet were bare and his clothes tattered. His eyes had the dull stare of a man once proud and free, but now deprived of the will to maintain his own gentle life-style.

The Pygmies are central Africa's oldest known surviving people and in the 1930s about 35,000 proudly lived in the Itiru Forest of the eastern Congo, now called Zaire. By 1957 their population had fallen to 25,000.

During the fifties, the Pygmies' ancestral forest was wastefully chopped down by lumber industrialists, robbing them of the vegetation and game they depended upon for survival. Consequently, the people were forced into the blistering sun to which they were unaccustomed. Large plantations closed in on their environment. National parks and game reserves were established, but no land was set aside to aid the Pygmy societies in their struggle for survival. Tourists brought contagious diseases to which the Pygmies had no immunity, and as a result their population continued to decline.

In 1960 the Belgian Congo received political independence, becoming the nation of Zaire. This political change brought civil war for which the nonaggressive Pygmies were the first to suffer and their number rapidly dwindled to 15,000. They became victims of new burdens such as paying income taxes, being drafted into the Zaire army, and further loss of cultural identity. By 1975 their size numbered some 3,800.

The Pygmies have a warm and gentle life-style with a dignified moral code which forbids killing, lying, theft, devil worship, sorcery, disrespect for elders, and blasphemy. They do not engage in cannibalism, mutilation, ritual murder, intertribal war, initiation ordeals, or other cruel customs sometimes associated with equatorial Africa.

FORM C

Teacher Record

STUDENT RECORD SUMMARY SHEET

Student _____ Grade _____ Sex _____ Age _____
yrs. mos.

School _____ Administered by _____ Date _____

Grade	Word Lists	Graded Passages			Estimated Levels
	% of words correct	WR Form ____	Comp. Form ____	Listen. Form ____	
Primer					
1					
2					Grade
3					Independent _____
4					Instructional _____
5					Frustration _____
6					Listening _____
7					
8					
9					

Check consistent oral reading difficulties:

____ word-by-word reading

____ omissions

____ substitutions

____ corrections

____ repetitions

____ reversals

____ inattention to punctuation

____ word inserts

____ requests word help

Check consistent word recognition difficulties:

____ single consonants

____ consonant clusters

____ long vowels

____ short vowels

____ vowel digraphs

____ diphthongs

____ syllabication

____ use of context

____ basic sight

____ grade level sight

Check consistent comprehension difficulties:

____ main idea

____ factual

____ terminology

____ cause and effect

____ inferential

____ drawing conclusions

____ retelling

Description of Reading Behaviors:

_____

_____

_____

_____

QUALITATIVE ANALYSIS SUMMARY SHEET

FORM _____

Student _____ Grade _____ Sex _____ Age _____
                                                                                              yrs. mos.

Level	Word in Text	What Child Read	Sampling of Miscues	
			Meaning Change	Nature of Miscue*

Summary and Comments _____
_____
_____
_____
_____
_____
_____

*A miscue may be lack of knowledge of any of the following: basic sight words; grade level sight vocabulary; consonant sounds; vowel sounds; blends; digraphs; diphthongs; structural analysis of roots, affixes, possessives, plurals, word families, compound words, accent, and syllabication rules. For complete definitions and suggestions for remediation of each of these miscues, refer to Ekwall (1985).

(Student Booklet page 100)

(Primer)	(1)	(2)
1. about _____	1. ice _____	1. goose _____
2. can _____	2. before _____	2. mouse _____
3. who _____	3. another _____	3. library _____
4. with _____	4. children _____	4. teacher _____
5. some _____	5. stopped _____	5. kite _____
6. goat _____	6. hurry _____	6. cart _____
7. out _____	7. drop _____	7. different _____
8. trees _____	8. friend _____	8. anyone _____
9. father _____	9. balloon _____	9. feather _____
10. red _____	10. when _____	10. pie _____
11. green _____	11. where _____	11. sidewalk _____
12. make _____	12. those _____	12. straight _____
13. is _____	13. picnic _____	13. telephone _____
14. yes _____	14. laugh _____	14. clean _____
15. saw _____	15. farm _____	15. remember _____
16. get _____	16. airplane _____	16. wood _____
17. ball _____	17. tomorrow _____	17. summer _____
18. and _____	18. wagon _____	18. bell _____
19. down _____	19. made _____	19. gun _____
20. are _____	20. surprise _____	20. matter _____

(Student Booklet page 101)

(3)

1. clap _____
2. fright _____
3. diamond _____
4. silence _____
5. nurse _____
6. wiggle _____
7. precious _____
8. salt _____
9. bread _____
10. breath _____
11. fellow _____
12. several _____
13. unusual _____
14. overhead _____
15. driven _____
16. fool _____
17. darkness _____
18. honor _____
19. screen _____
20. they'll _____

(4)

1. canoe _____
2. hasn't _____
3. dozen _____
4. motion _____
5. pride _____
6. vicious _____
7. concern _____
8. harvest _____
9. sample _____
10. official _____
11. windshield _____
12. human _____
13. humor _____
14. decorate _____
15. slender _____
16. seventh _____
17. parachute _____
18. good-bye _____
19. dignity _____
20. trudge _____

(Student Booklet page 102)

(5)

1. prevent_____
2. kindle_____
3. grease_____
4. typical_____
5. foam_____
6. blur_____
7. mumps_____
8. telegram_____
9. vision_____
10. sandal_____
11. argument_____
12. hail_____
13. halt_____
14. region_____
15. manager_____
16. sleet_____
17. yarn_____
18. parallel_____
19. coconut_____
20. dissolve_____

(6)

1. midstream_____
2. lens_____
3. bail_____
4. college_____
5. failure_____
6. falter_____
7. width_____
8. graceful_____
9. somewhat_____
10. privacy_____
11. microphone_____
12. particle_____
13. clutter_____
14. applaud_____
15. vapor_____
16. reluctant_____
17. contract_____
18. nephew_____
19. insurance_____
20. fund_____

Primer (50 words   8 sent.)

Examiner's Introduction
(Student Booklet page 103):   Please read this story about a child who imagines some unusual things.

Look! It is me!

I can run as fast as a train!

I can jump over a big tall tree!

I can ride my bike as fast as a running goat!

I can see very little things far away.

I can put on a good show!

Yes, I am something!

Comprehension Questions and Possible Answers

(mi)   1. What is this story about?
(The special kid, Super kid, etc.)

(f)   2. What does the child mean by saying, "I can run as fast as a train"?
(can run very fast)

(f)   3. How high can this child jump?
(over a big tall tree)

(t)   4. How fast can the child ride the bike?
(as fast as a running goat)

(t)   5. What is meant by the word over?
(above)

(f)   6. What kind of things can the child see far away?
(very little things)

Miscue Count:

O____I____S____A____REP____REV____

Scoring Guide	
Word Rec.	Comp.
IND 0–1	IND 0
INST 2–3	INST 1–2
FRUST 5+	FRUST 3+

Level 1 (76 words 9 sent.)

Examiner's Introduction (Student Booklet page 104): Imagine what your Mom would say if you brought every animal you saw home to live in your house. Please read about this nonsense zoo.

I found a lost baby turtle. I took him home so he could live in my house. A friend gave me his prize rabbit. I took the rabbit home to live in my house.

I found a lost duck so I took her home too. I saw a little, cold blackbird and took him home. Then, I saw a cow who looked so sad. I took her home!

But Mom said, "No! No! Not a cow!"

Comprehension Questions and Possible Answers

(mi) 1. What is the child in this story doing?
(collecting stray animals)

(f) 2. What animal did the child find first?
(lost baby turtle)

(t) 3. What is meant by the phrase, "a prize rabbit"?
(the best one, one which wins honors)

(f) 4. How did the cow look?
(so sad)

(f) 5. Name the animals that the child in the story took home.
(turtle, rabbit, duck, blackbird, cow)

(inf) 6. What is said in the story which makes you think Mother didn't want a cow in the house?
(Stated: She said, "No! No! Not a cow!")

Miscue Count:

O___ I___ S___ A___ REP___ REV___

Scoring Guide	
Word Rec.	Comp.
IND 0–1	IND 0
INST 3–4	INST 1–2
FRUST 8+	FRUST 3+

Form C / Teacher Record / Graded Paragraphs

**Examiner's Introduction
(Student Booklet page 105):** If your pet has ever been hurt or injured, you will understand how the child in the next story feels. Please read this story.

"Look out, you'll get hit!" I yelled as Shep ran across the busy road. "Thud!" was the noise I heard, and then I saw my pup lying in the street. "Oh, no!" I shouted. I felt scared inside.

"Shep is my best friend!" I wanted to cry out. I knew that he was hurt, but he'd be all right if I could get help fast. I knew I had to be brave.

"Mom! Dad!" I yelled as I ran straight home. I tried to fight back the tears. But they started rolling down my face anyway as I blasted through the door. "Shep has been hit, and he's badly hurt!" I cried out. "Please hurry and help him!"

**Comprehension Questions
and Possible Answers**

(mi) 1. In this story, what happens to the child's dog?
(gets hit on a busy road)

(f) 2. When the child first saw the hurt pet, how did the child feel?
(scared inside)

(t) 3. What is meant by the phrase, "fight back the tears"?
(to try to keep from crying)

(f) 4. Where did the child run to get help?
(ran straight home)

(ce) 5. What would happen if the child could get help fast?
(Shep would be all right.)

(inf) 6. What does the child say to make you think he loved the dog?
(Stated: Shep is my best friend.)

Miscue Count:

O____I____S____A____REP____REV____

Scoring Guide	
Word Rec.	Comp.
IND 1	IND 0
INST 6	INST 1–2
FRUST 12+	FRUST 3+

**Examiner's Introduction
(Student Booklet page 106):**

This is a story of a new boy who has a problem and thinks of an ingenious way to solve his problem. Please read how he sets out to do this.

FOR NEIGHBORHOOD TIGERS ONLY! KNOCK ONE THOUSAND TIMES AND SAY THE SECRET WORD BEFORE ENTERING!

These were the signs which Jack read as he stood outside the neighborhood clubhouse. Jack was a new boy, and he really wanted to belong to the club. "How can I get the kids to agree to let me belong?" he thought. Suddenly he dashed home and soon returned with a bucket of yellow paint, one of black, and several brushes. He began pounding on the clubhouse door.

"I'm knocking a thousand times!" he shouted. "I don't know the secret word," he declared, "but I have something important to tell everyone! I'm the new boy," he explained. "Since the name of your club is 'Tigers,' I thought you might want to paint your clubhouse yellow with black stripes!"

All the kids thought this was a great idea and quickly invited Jack to belong!

**Comprehension Questions
and Possible Answers**

(mi) 1. Why does Jack want to belong to the club?
      (He is the new boy and wants to make friends.)

(f)   2. Where was Jack standing when he read the signs?
      (outside the clubhouse)

(t)   3. In the sentence, "how can I get the kids to agree to let me belong," what is meant by the word *belong*?
      (consent to his membership in the club)

(f)   4. What did Jack dash home to get?
      (yellow and black paint and several brushes)

(t)   5. What is meant by the phrase, "he explained"?
      (He told all about something.)

(ce) 6. Why did Jack finally knock on the clubhouse door?
      (He had something to tell everyone.)

(ce) 7. Why did the kids quickly invite Jack to belong?
      (They thought he had a great idea.)

(inf) 8. What is said in the story that makes you think Jack was lonely and eager to make friends?
(Stated: He was a new boy, and he wanted to belong to the neighborhood clubhouse.)

Miscue Count:

O____ I____ S____ A____ REP____ REV____

Scoring Guide			
Word Rec.		Comp.	
IND	1–2	IND	0–1
INST	7–8	INST	2
FRUST	15+	FRUST	4+

Level 4 (144 words   12 sent.)

Examiner's Introduction (Student Booklet page 107):

If you ever had a pet that you loved, then you will understand how Jody felt about Gabilan in John Steinbeck's book, *The Red Pony*. In the winter Gabilan catches pneumonia and things take a turn for the worse. Please read a retelling of one of the incidents from this memorable book.

Jody was so worried that he didn't even care to eat. He had stayed in the barn all day to take care of his sick pony, Gabilan. The pony's condition was growing worse as his breathing grew louder and harder.

At nightfall Jody brought a blanket from the house so he could sleep near Gabilan. In the middle of the night a wind whipped around the barn and blew the door open.

At dawn Jody awakened to the banging of the barn door. Gabilan was gone! In alarm he ran from the barn following the pony's tracks. Looking upward he saw buzzards, the birds of death, flying overhead. Jody stood still, then ran to the top of a small hill. In a clearing below, he saw something that filled his heart with anger and hate. A buzzard was perched on his dying pony's head.

Comprehension Questions and Possible Answers

(mi)   1. In this passage, what was wrong with Jody's colt?
(Gabilan was sick and getting worse.)

(t)   2. In this story, what is meant by the phrase, "pony's condition"?
(Gabilan's poor health)

(ce)   3. Why did Jody take a blanket from the house?
(so he could sleep near Gabilan)

(f)   4. What awakened Jody at dawn?
(the banging of the barn door)

(t)   5. What is meant by the phrase "at dawn"?
(at sunrise, at the start of the day)

(ce)   6. Why was the barn door banging?
(In the middle of the night a wind whipped around the barn and blew the door open.)

(f)   7. How did Jody try to find his pony?
(He followed the pony's tracks.)

(inf)   8. What is said in the story that makes you think Jody feared his pony might be dead?
(Stated: Looking upward he saw buzzards, the birds of death, flying overhead.)

Miscue Count:

O____ I____ S____ A____ REP____ REV____

Scoring Guide	
Word Rec.	Comp.
IND 1–2	IND 0–1
INST 7–8	INST 2
FRUST 15+	FRUST 4+

**Examiner's Introduction
(Student Booklet page 108):**

This is a story about one outstanding auto racer. The following information was derived from an article entitled, "Woman Drag Racer After Speed Record," appearing in a 1975 issue of *The Christian Science Monitor*.

"I want to be the fastest woman driver in the world," stated Shirley Muldowney. "I'd really like to go 500 miles per hour, but I'll be happy to go 400 this year and try for 500 next year," she quickly added.

Shirley, nicknamed Cha Cha, is presently the only woman licensed to drive Top Fuel cars. These cars are the fastest, the most powerful, and among the most carefully built machines in the car racing sport. Not only is she licensed to drive Top Fuel cars, but she is now one of the top challengers in the country. She has established a top speed of 241.58 miles per hour. No Top Fuel driver has reached a speed of over 250 miles per hour.

Shirley has a great deal of energy, determination, and nerve. She is confident that she can drive her car to victory. It is characteristic of her to accomplish about anything she sets out to do. A good friend has said, "It's been a long time since people thought of her just as a woman who drives race cars. She's a top driver who just happens to be a woman!"

**Comprehension Questions
and Possible Answers**

(mi) 1. What is unusual about Shirley Muldowney's career?
(She is the only woman licensed to drive Top Fuel cars.)

(f) 2. What does Shirley state to be her goal?
(She wants to be the fastest woman driver in the world by going 500 miles per hour.)

(t) 3. What is meant by the word *determination*?
(strong will to accomplish something)

(f) 4. What is special about Top Fuel cars in the racing sport?
(the fastest, most powerful, and among the most carefully built)

(ce) 5. Why is Shirley one of the top challengers in the country?
(She has established a top speed of 241.58 miles per hour.)

(t) 6. What is meant by the word *characteristic*?
(something which describes that particular person)

(ce) 7. Why don't people think of Shirley as just a woman who drives cars?
(She's a top driver.)

(con) 8. What is said in this story that makes you think Shirley will do well as a Top Fuel driver? (Stated: She has energy, determination, and nerve; she is confident she can win races; she accomplishes what she sets out to do.)

Miscue Count:

O____ I____ S____ A____ REP____ REV____

Scoring Guide	
Word Rec.	Comp.
IND 2	IND 0–1
INST 9	INST 2
FRUST 18+	FRUST 4+

Level 6 (189 words 13 sent.)

**Examiner's Introduction
(Student Booklet page 109):** You are about to read of a very dedicated and famous black surgeon who defied medical tradition and performed unusual surgery before the 1900s. The following information was derived from a book entitled, *Black Pioneers of Science and Invention*, by Louis Haber.

James Cornish lay wounded on the saloon floor! "He's been stabbed in the chest!" shouted one horrified bystander. "Someone get him to a hospital!" another shouted.

It was a hot and humid day in Chicago in 1893. Cornish arrived at the hospital with a one-inch knife wound in his chest, dangerously near his heart. Dr. Daniel Hale Williams was called in to operate.

In those days when blood transfusions and antibiotics were unknown, chest surgery was rarely attempted since it meant a high risk of death. As Dr. Williams began to operate, he found that the stab wound had cut the heart and the sac around the heart. Dr. Williams then made history by becoming the first surgeon to successfully operate on the human heart.

Dr. Williams did not release this information for three and a half years. When he did, the newspaper headline read, "Sewed Up His Heart," and the news became known to the entire world. Not only had Cornish been discharged from the hospital a well man, but he lived fifty years after his surgery. Cornish even outlived the surgeon who had saved his life.

**Comprehension Questions
and Possible Answers**

(mi) 1. What was Dr. Daniel Williams' unusual accomplishment?
(performed heart surgery before the days of modern medicine)

(f) 2. Where was Cornish's wound?
(in the chest, dangerously near his heart)

(t) 3. What is meant by the word *rarely*?
(not very often)

(ce) 4. When Dr. Williams found that the heart had been cut, what did he do?
(sewed it up)

(t) 5. What is meant by the phrase, "release this information"?
(give the news to the papers)

(ce) 6. What happened when Williams finally released the news?
(Newspapers printed the story, and the news became known to the entire world.)

(f) 7. How long did Cornish live after his surgery?
(fifty years)

(inf) 8. What is said in this story that makes you think chest surgery was so unusual in those days?
(Stated: Blood transfusions and antibiotics were unknown, causing high risk of death.)

Miscue Count:

O___ I___ S___ A___ REP___ REV___

Level 7 (241 words   15 sent.)

**Examiner's Introduction
(Student Booklet page 110):** Maia Wojciechowska's book, *Tuned Out*, is a realistic exposure of the drug scene and its harmful effects. Please read a retelling of one of the incidents from this memorable book.

Jim was sixteen years old, and he thought more of his older brother, Kevin, than anyone else. He had informed all his friends that he'd not see them during the summer because he would be spending all his time with Kevin. It would be a terrific summer because Kevin was the greatest guy in the world.

But when Kevin arrived home from his first year at college something was different about him; he seemed unsettled, stayed confined to his room, and requested that Jim not disturb him. He wasn't interested in talking over old times. In fact, everything seemed to bore him.

Soon Jim discovered that Kevin had changed. Kevin smoked grass and spent his days beating the streets looking for LSD. Jim was stunned, bewildered, and to make things worse, it seemed to him that their parents didn't notice any unusual change in Kevin's personality.

Then one evening that inevitable occurrence which goes along with the drug scene happened. Kevin had taken the LSD near the time their folks left the house. It wasn't long before Jim found his brother convulsing, writhing on the floor, hallucinating, and unconsciously screaming out crazy things.

It was a frightful experience for Jim to see Kevin in such torture. He was terrorized with fear as he hurled himself on top of Kevin, grabbing at his arms in an attempt to keep his brother from injuring himself. He knew he had to get help immediately!

**Comprehension Questions
and Possible Answers**

(mi) 1. Why was Jim so concerned about his brother?
(He had discovered that Kevin was taking drugs.)

(ce) 2. Why did Jim inform his friends that he'd not see them during the summer?
(He wanted to spend all his time with his brother, Kevin.)

(f) 3. How did Jim feel when he discovered that Kevin was taking drugs?
(stunned, bewildered)

(t) 4. What is meant by the phrase, "beating the streets"?
(to search thoroughly by walking around the streets)

(t) 5. What is meant by an "inevitable occurrence"?
(something unavoidable)

(ce) 6. How did the LSD affect Kevin?
(convulsing, writhing, hallucinating, screaming)

(ce) 7. Why did Jim throw himself on top of his brother?
(to keep Kevin from injuring himself)

(con) 8. What is said in the story that makes you think Kevin's parents didn't know about his problem?
(Stated: Jim thought they hadn't noticed; they had left the house)

Miscue Count:

O____ I____ S____ A____ REP____ REV____

Scoring Guide		
Word Rec.		Comp.
IND	2–3	IND	0–1
INST	13	INST	2
FRUST	26 +	FRUST	4 +

**Examiner's Introduction
(Student Booklet page 111):**

The next selection you are to read is about vampires. At one time in our history vampires and other supernatural beings were believed to exist. The following information was derived from an article entitled, "Vampires," from *Man, Myth, and Magic: An Illustrated Encyclopedia of the Supernatural.*

"I am . . . Dracula," murmured a black-caped, fanged-toothed, pointed-eared monster. "I never drink . . . wine," he declared as movie-goers sat petrified in their seats.

In 1931, a novel by Irish author Bram Stoker became vividly alive on the movie screen as thousands flocked to see this re-creation of the vampire superstition which dates back to the sixteenth century.

According to the novel, a vampire looks pale, lean, and has a death-like icy touch. His eyes gleam or flash red, his ears are pointed like those of a werewolf, and his fingernails are curled and sharp. Some tales describe him as skeletal and often dressed in a black costume. His limited diet of blood gives him a foul-smelling breath. Old legends depict him with only one nostril and a barbed tongue. These creatures have the power to change their form into a cloud of mist or a bizarre nocturnal animal.

Despite modern disbelief in vampires, during the seventeenth century many thought they existed. It was believed that once a person died he could possibly return as a vampire. A corpse was often fastened in its grave with pegs or iron skewers to prevent a potential vampire from escaping.

Since the vampire was dormant during the day, graves were examined for small holes through which the monster could escape. If a grave was discovered with such holes, vampire hunters would remove the body and destroy it. This procedure took place during the daytime hours and all the hunters returned to their homes before sunset.

**Comprehension Questions
and Possible Answers**

(mi) 1. What is the main idea of this article?
(Belief in vampires existed in the 16th and 17th centuries.)

(f) 2. What are a vampire's eyes supposed to look like?
(gleaming or flashing red)

(f) 3. How did old legends describe a vampire?
(one nostril and a barbed tongue)

(t) 4. What is meant by the phrase, "bizarre animal"?
(unique or strange)

(t)   5. What is meant by the phrase, "dormant during the day"?
(was not dangerous in the daytime)

(ce)   6. Why were iron skewers used to fasten a corpse to its grave?
(to prevent it from escaping)

(ce)   7. Why were the graves examined during the day?
(There was less danger as vampires slept during the day.)

(con) 8. What is said in this story that makes you think people in the 16th and 17th centuries believed in and feared vampires?
(Stated: They fastened corpses in their graves with iron skewers; they searched graves for perforations and if holes were found they destroyed the corpse.)

Miscue Count:

O____ I____ S____ A____ REP____ REV____

Scoring Guide			
Word Rec.		Comp.	
IND	3	IND	0–1
INST	15	INST	2
FRUST	30+	FRUST	4+

**Examiner's Introduction
(Student Booklet page 112):** Jean-Pierre Haller, a Belgian explorer and author, went to the Belgian Congo in 1957 to assist the Pygmies in their dramatic struggle for survival. The following passage was derived from an article entitled, "To Save A People."

A young Pygmy stood in the parching equatorial African sun. He stood but five feet tall and his stature was bent from hard labor. His skin was golden brown and his hair was short and curled tightly to his head. His feet were bare and his clothes tattered. His eyes had the dull stare of a man once proud and free, but now deprived of the will to maintain his own gentle life-style.

The Pygmies are central Africa's oldest known surviving people and in the 1930's about 35,000 proudly lived in the Itiru Forest of the eastern Congo, now called Zaire. By 1957 their population had fallen to 25,000.

During the fifties, the Pygmies' ancestral forest was wastefully chopped down by lumber industrialists, robbing them of the vegetation and game they depended upon for survival. Consequently, the people were forced into the blistering sun to which they were unaccustomed. Large plantations closed in on their environment. National parks and game reserves were established, but no land was set aside to aid the Pygmy societies in their struggle for survival. Tourists brought contagious diseases to which the Pygmies had no immunity, and as a result their population continued to decline.

In 1960 the Belgian Congo received political independence, becoming the nation of Zaire. This political change brought civil war for which the nonaggressive Pygmies were the first to suffer and their number rapidly dwindled to 15,000. They became victims of new burdens such as paying income taxes, being drafted into the Zaire army, and further loss of cultural identity. By 1975 their size numbered some 3,800.

The Pygmies have a warm and gentle life-style with a dignified moral code which forbids killing, lying, theft, devil worship, sorcery, disrespect for elders, and blasphemy. They do not engage in cannibalism, mutilation, ritual murder, intertribal war, initiation ordeals, or other cruel customs sometimes associated with equatorial Africa.

Comprehension Questions and Possible Answers

(mi) 1. What is the main idea of this passage?
      (This Pygmy tribe is facing near extinction.)

(f)   2. Where is the Itiru Forest?
      (eastern Congo, now called Zaire)

(ce) 3. What happened to the Pygmy society when their forests were chopped down?
      (They were robbed of the vegetation and game they depended upon for survival.)

(t)   4. What is meant by the word *immunity*?
      (condition of being able to resist a particular disease)

(f)   5. What did tourists bring to the Pygmies?
      (contagious diseases)

(t)   6. What is meant by the phrase, "nonaggressive Pygmies"?
      (nonhostile, nonwarlike)

(ce) 7. How were the Pygmies affected when the Belgian Congo received political independence?
      (Civil war and new suffering for the Pygmies)

(con) 8. What is said in this story that makes you think no one cared enough to protect the Pygmies' rights?
      (Stated: Lumber industrialists wastefully chopped down the Pygmies' forests; parks and game reserves were set aside but no land was saved for the Pygmies.)

Miscue Count:

O____ I____ S____ A____ REP____ REV____

Scoring Guide			
Word Rec.		Comp.	
IND	3–4	IND	0–1
INST	18	INST	2
FRUST	36+	FRUST	4+

CLASS RECORD SUMMARY SHEET

Student	Date	Reading Level Scores			Listening Level	Assigned Reading Text	Comments
		Ind.	Inst.	Frust.			

REFERENCES

Three sets of references are provided in this section. They consist of references for teachers on the correction and remediation of reading problems, references cited in the inventory, and references which provided the information necessary to write the student passages.

References on Correction and Remediation

Following these bibliographic entries on reading instruction, there is a listing of common reading problems and the pages where information may be obtained on how to solve such problems.

Aukerman, R. C. & Aukerman, L. R. *How do I teach reading?* New York: John Wiley & Sons, Inc., 1981.

Baumann, J. F. & Johnson, D. D. (Eds.). *Reading instruction and the beginning teacher: A practical guide.* Minneapolis: Burgess Publishing Co., 1984.

Bixby, Mary; Crenshaw, Shirley; Crowley, Paul; Gilles, Carol; Henrichs, Margaret; Pyle, Donelle; and Waters, Frances. *Strategies that make sense: Invitations to literacy for secondary students.* Columbia, Missouri: Mid-Missouri TAWL, 1983.

Bond, G. L., Tinker, M. A., Wasson, B. B. & Wasson, J. B. *Reading difficulties: Their diagnosis and correction* (5th ed.). Englewood Cliffs, New Jersey: Prentice-Hall, Inc., 1984.

Brown, D. A. *Reading diagnosis and remediation.* Englewood Cliffs, New Jersey: Prentice-Hall, Inc., 1982.

Collins-Cheek, M. & Cheek, E. H. *Diagnostic-prescriptive reading instruction* (2nd ed.). Dubuque, Iowa: Wm. C. Brown Publishers, 1984.

Cooper, D. J., Warncke, E. W., Ramstad, P. A. & Shipman, D. A. *The what and how of reading instruction.* Columbus, Ohio: Charles E. Merrill, 1979.

Cooper, J. and Worden, T. W. *The classroom reading program in the elementary school.* New York: Macmillan Publishing Co., 1983.

Dallman, M., Rouch, R. L., Char, L.Y.C., & DeBoer, J. J. *The teaching of reading* (6th ed.). New York: Holt, Rinehart and Winston, 1982.

Dechant, E. V. *Improving the teaching of reading* (3rd ed.). Englewood Cliffs, New Jersey: Prentice-Hall Inc., 1982.

Ekwall, E. E. *Locating and correcting reading difficulties* (4th ed.). Columbus, Ohio: Charles E. Merrill, 1985.

Ekwall, E. E. & Shanker, J. L. *Diagnosis and remediation of the disabled reader* (2nd ed.). Boston: Allyn and Bacon, Inc., 1983.

Goodman, Yetta M.; Burke, Carolyn; and Sherman, Barry. *Reading strategies: Focus on comprehension.* New York: Holt, Rinehart and Winston, 1980.

Heilman, A. W., Blair, T. R., & Rupley, W. H. *Principles and practices of teaching reading* (5th ed.). Columbus, Ohio: Charles E. Merrill Publishing Co., 1981.

Hornsby, B. & Shear, F. *Alpha to omega.* Exeter, N. H.: Heinemann Educational Books, 1979.

Johnson, D. D. & Moe, A. J. *The Ginn word book for teachers: A basic lexicon.* Lexington, Mass.: Ginn and Company, 1983.

Johnson, D. D. & Pearson, P. D. *Teaching reading vocabulary* (2nd ed.). New York: Holt, Rinehart and Winston, 1984.

Karlin, R. *Teaching elementary reading: Principles and strategies* (3rd ed.). New York: Harcourt Brace Jovanovich, Inc., 1980.

Newman, Judith M. *Whole language activities.* Halifax, Nova Scotia: Department of Education, Dalhousie University, 1983.

Pearson, P. D. and Johnson, D. D. *Teaching reading comprehension.* New York: Holt, Rinehart and Winston, 1978.

Searfoss, L. W. & Readence, J. E. *Helping children learn to read.* Englewood Cliffs, New Jersey: Prentice-Hall, Inc., 1985.

Smith, N. B. & Robinson, H. A. *Reading instruction for today's children.* (2nd ed.). Englewood Cliffs, New Jersey: Prentice-Hall, Inc., 1980.

Spache, G. D. *Diagnosing and correcting reading disabilities* (2nd ed.). Boston: Allyn and Bacon, Inc., 1981.

Wilson, R. M. *Diagnostic and remedial reading for classroom and clinic* (5th ed.). Columbus, Ohio: Charles E. Merrill Publishing Co., 1985.

Zintz, M. V. *Corrective Reading* (4th ed.). Dubuque, Iowa: Wm. C. Brown Company Publishers, 1981.

Common Reading Problems

1. *Aided Words*

   Bond, Tinker, Wasson and Wasson Ch. 11
   Dechant pp. 372–373
   Spache p. 144

2. *Vocabulary*

   Baumann and Johnson Ch. 1, 2, 3
   Johnson and Pearson Ch. 2, 3, 6
   Searfoss and Readence Ch. 6

3. *Comprehension*

   Aukerman and Aukerman   pp. 275–324
   Baumann and Johnson   Ch. 4 & 5
   Bixby, Crenshaw, Crowley, Gilles, Henrichs, Pyle and Waters
   Bond, Tinker, Wasson and Wasson   Ch. 14, 15
   Cooper, Warncke, Ramstad and Shipman   pp. 3–53
   Collins-Cheek and Cheek   Ch. 11
   Dechant   Ch. 13
   Ekwall and Shanker   Ch. 6
   Goodman, Burke, and Sherman
   Heilman, Blair and Rupley   Ch. 8
   Karlin   Ch. 7
   Newman
   Pearson and Johnson
   Smith and Robinson   Ch. 8
   Wilson   Ch. 10
   Zintz   Ch. 11

4. *Hesitations*

   Bond, Tinker, Wasson and Wasson   pp. 320–325
   Brown   pp. 63–64
   Dechant   pp. 375–76

5. *Insertions*

   Collins-Cheek and Cheek   p. 83
   Dechant   pp. 368–69

6. *Omissions*

   Collins-Cheek and Cheek   p. 83
   Dechant   pp. 368–69

7. *Repetitions*

   Dechant   pp. 371–372
   Ekwall and Shanker   pp. 393–400

8. *Reversals*

   Bond, Tinker and Wasson   pp. 284–285
   Ekwall and Shanker   p. 397
   Spache   pp. 144–145, 148
   Zintz   pp. 86–88

9. *Substitutions*

   Collins-Cheek and Cheek   p. 83
   Dechant   p. 370
   Ekwall and Shanker   pp. 393–400

References Cited in the Text

Anderson, W. W. Focus on measurement and evaluation—Commercial reading inventories: A comparative review. *Reading World,* December 1977, 99–104.

Arbuthnot, M. H., & Sutherland, Z. *Children and books* (4th ed.). Glenview, Ill.: Scott Foresman, 1972.

Beldin, H. O. Informal reading testing: Historical review and review of the research. In W. Durr (Ed.), *Reading difficulties: Diagnosis, correction and remediation.* Newark, Del.: International Reading Association, 1970.

Ekwall, E. E. Informal reading inventories: The instructional level. *The Reading Teacher*, April 1976a, *29*, 662–665.

⸻. *Diagnosis and remediation of the disabled reader.* Boston: Allyn & Bacon, 1976b.

⸻. *Locating and correcting reading difficulties* (4th ed.). Columbus, Ohio: Charles E. Merrill, 1985.

Freiberger, R. *The New York Times report on teenage reading tastes and habits.* New York: A New York Times Company Survey, 1973.

Goodman, K. S. (Ed.). *Miscue analysis: Application to reading instruction.* Urbana, Ill.: ERIC Clearinghouse on Reading and Communication Skills, National Council of Teachers of English, 1973.

Goodman, Y., & Burke, C. *Reading miscue inventory.* New York: Macmillan, 1972.

Harris, A. J. Some new developments in readability. In John E. Merritt (Ed.), *New horizons in reading.* Newark, Del.: International Reading Association, 1976.

Harris, A. J., & Jacobson, M. D. *Basic elementary reading vocabularies.* The First R Series. New York: Macmillan, 1972.

Harris, A. J., & Sipay, E. R. *How to increase reading ability (6th ed.).* New York: David McKay, 1975.

Johnson, M. S., & Kress, R. A. *Informal reading inventories.* Newark, Del.: International Reading Association, 1965.

Kujoth, J. S. *Reading interests of children and young adults.* Metuchen, N. J.: The Scarecrow Press, 1970.

Pikulski, J. A critical review: Informal reading inventories. *The Reading Teacher*, November 1974, *28*, 141–151.

Powell, W. R. Reappraising the criteria for interpreting informal reading inventories. In D. DeBoer (Ed.), *Reading diagnosis and evaluation.* Newark, Del.: International Reading Association, 1970.

Powell, W. R., & Dunkeld, C. G. Validity of the IRI reading levels. *Elementary English*, October 1971, *48*, 637–642.

Sanders, N. M. *Classroom questions: What kinds?* New York: Harper & Row, 1966.

Spache, G. D. *Good reading for poor readers.* Champaign, Ill.: Garrard Publishing, 1974.

Tanyzer, H., & Karl, J. *Reading children's books and our pluralistic society.* Newark, Del.: International Reading Association, 1972.

Tuinman, J. J. Asking reading-dependent questions. *Journal of Reading*, February 1971, *14*, 289–292, 336.

Valmont, W. J. Creating questions for informal reading inventories. *The Reading Teacher*, March 1972, *25*, 509–512.

References for Passage Content

Borstein, L. Woman drag racer after speed record. *The Christian Science Monitor*, Midwestern Edition, July 31, 1975.

Burnford, S. *The incredible journey*. Boston: Little, Brown, 1961.

Gentry, J. How one town solves pollution and saves water. *The Plain Truth: A Magazine of Understanding*, January 1973, 30–35.

Gott, L. Who's that polluting my world? *The Plain Truth, A Magazine of Understanding*, January 1973, 25–29.

Haber, L. *Black pioneers of science and invention*. New York: Harcourt Brace Jovanovich, 1970.

Henry, M. *Justin Morgan had a horse*. New York: Rand McNally, 1972.

Hill, D. Vampires. In Richard Cavendish (Ed.), *Man, myth, and magic: An illustrated encyclopedia of the supernatural* (Vol. 21). New York: Marshall Cavendish Corp., 1970. Pp. 2922–28.

Hinton, S. E. *The outsiders*. New York: The Viking Press, 1969.

Hoeh, H. L. To save a people. *The Plain Truth, A Magazine of Understanding*, January 1975, 9–15.

Huxley, F. Zombies. In Richard Cavendish (Ed.), *Man, myth, and magic: An illustrated encyclopedia of the supernatural* (Vol. 22). New York: Marshall Cavendish Corp., 1970. Pp. 3095–96.

Maple, E. East Anglican and Essex witches. In Richard Cavendish (Ed.), *Man, myth, and magic: An illustrated encyclopedia of the supernatural* (Vol. 6). New York: Marshall Cavendish Corp., 1970. Pp. 753–758.

McKay, R. *Dave's song*. New York: Meredith Press, 1969.

Michaud, S., & Michaud, R. Trek to the lofty Hunza and beyond. *National Geographic*, November 1975, 647–668.

Robyn Smith. *The Lincoln library of sports champions* (Vol. 12). Columbus, Ohio: Sports Resources Co., 1974. Pp. 32–35.

Sportswomanlike conduct. *Newsweek*, June 3, 1974, pp. 50–55.

Steinbeck, J. *The red pony*. New York: The Viking Press, 1966.

Wojciechowska, M. *Tuned out*. New York: Harper & Row, 1968.

34   5